BY JEAN FRENETTE

BEYOND KICKING

A COMPLETE GUIDE TO STRETCHING AND KICKING

Jean Frenette's Beyond karate
Kicking by Jean Frenette

 Published by I&I SPORTS SUPPLY
ISBN 978-0-934489-96-6

BY JEAN FRENETTE

BEYOND KICKING

A COMPLETE GUIDE TO STRETCHING AND KICKING

Table of Contents

CHAPTER 1

That Championship Workout

I have a friend who pound-for-pound could be one of the best, most powerful martial artists the world has ever seen. His love for the arts is unswerving, his diligence toward spending time in the training hall a quality to be admired even by the best of modern champions. In short, he has the title "No. 1" written all over him.

But, the sad fact is, he may be the greatest martial artist you'll never hear about. While he appears to possess a world of physical potential, he lacks an understanding of what it ultimately takes to become a martial arts champion.

A concrete plan.

You see, he is among a growing number of martial artists who think the road to international stardom begins and ends on the arena floor, with a center judge wearing gray slacks and red tie holding a victor's arm high into the air for all to see. They think that:

- Stretching should be reserved for beginners;
- Weight training is the stuff of body builders;
- Only internal stylists should practice concentration and visualization exercises;
- Cardiovascular training is a concern for runners; and
- Proper diet should be practiced by those with a weight problem.

Well I'm here tell you they're dead wrong, and if you need proof go to a nationally rated tournament some time and watch those who fall by the wayside. They will be the ones whose moves, jumps and kicks lack strength and crispness; they are the ones whose weapons work lacks power and endurance; they are the ones who lose points on focus; they are the ones who can't finish a routine without huffing and puffing through their mouths.

They are the martial artists who think you can start practicing Friday for a tournament on Saturday. And they are the practitioners who leave without the hardware.

Many have asked that with the success of my first book, *Jean Frenette's Complete Guide to Stretching,* what is there left to say? My answer is plenty. While the first book gave you a comprehensive look at the need for stretching in the martial arts—from the philosophy and dangers of stretching, to programs for beginners through advanced—this book helps you establish a goal, develop a plan and follow it through to completion.

Just as there is more to martial arts than simply forms or fighting, there is more to preparing your body for competition than merely learning how to properly stretch.

With competition at today's tournaments keener than ever before, you must prepare yourself both mentally and physically for the battles that lay ahead. Therefore, you must devise a personal plan of attack that will put you in the best possible shape when the competition begins. Along with superstretching secrets, you'll learn how to use your flexibility to improve kicking technique; discover why weight training will add power to your forms; realize the benefits of concentration and visualization exercises; understand how a proper diet can lead to better performance; and put into practice a cardiovascular training program that will keep you going when the rest of the field has run out of gas.

Now don't think the subject of stretching has been neglected. It remains the most fundamental skill for any martial artist aspiring to make it to the top and it continues to occupy the yeomen's portion of this book. For those who graduated from the exercises illustrated in my first book, a brand new set of programs featured within these pages will test your mettle even further.

However, if you can master these superstretching secrets, you will gain an edge on the competition. I will take you to the ultimate level as far as flexibility is concerned; a no- holds-barred, try-them-if-you're-game approach to staying and remaining flexible.

A lot of martial artists think there's no need for a program of this magnitude. They think they can skip the hard work, show up at a tournament and win with little effort. That philosophy may hold true on the regional scene, but when it comes to the big national and international events, they won't stand a chance. Why? Because the top competitors know how to pace themselves throughout the year. They train around the most important three or four events each year. And sowhen it's time for them to be at their best, they are prepared.

You have to establish your goals in advance. Even if you compete every weekend, there are three or four "name" tournaments a year where you'll want to peak. You have to know when to train, how much to train and when to slow down and recuperate. To the champions, this is not a game; it is serious business and should be treated as such.

I must admit that this plan is not for everyone. It will take hours and days and weeks and months of hard work and discipline. But when the final battle has been waged and the referee raises your hand in triumph before all the world to see, you'll discover it was but a small price to pay for so great a success.

CHAPTER 2

Warming Up and Staying Strong

Next time you go to a professional sporting event, try arriving an hour or so early. What you'll find is that some of the world's fastest, strongest and most well-conditioned athletes are spending their pre-game hours warming up with general exercises.

Part of the painstaking process of being a top athlete, whether it be in the arena of baseball, football, basketball or martial arts—yes, martial arts—is knowing how to keep your body in peak condition. One of the best ways to insure peak performance is through a comprehensive warm-up and general exercise program that will prepare you for the upcoming competition.

When I began my martial arts training, I would always arrive at class 15-to-30 minutes early so I could stretch. This helped my muscles get warm and loose and kept the risk of injury at a minimum. The warm-up exercises should stress the areas of the body you'll be using that day, including the back, neck, shoulders, wrists, knees, ankles, calves and legs. Stretching is part of preparing your body for the rigors of martial arts training. You stretch your muscles when you kick, punch, jump, or assume a horse stance.

The reason for the warm-up is that once you get past the basics and into the general application of movement, you won't have to worry about potential injury. Your muscles will be awake and alive, your ligaments warmed up and ready for action.

A poor or insufficient stretching program is the main cause of injury among martial artists. The varied routines inherent in Japanese, Okinawan, Chinese or Korean styles place great and oftentimes unusual pressure on the body. Stretching in the martial arts is as important as working on the basics. Simply, if you don't stretch or properly warm up, you will get hurt—maybe not today or tomorrow, but surely sometime down the line.

As you become more proficient in your stretching program, your body will tell you when it has had enough. The body will give you a sign when it's a good pain—you can feel the stretch, feel the muscle expanding—and when it's a bad pain—a burning sensation followed by the feeling of someone taking a knife and slicing through the muscle. You will learn to listen to your body.

Remember, everyone's body is different: What someone else can do doesn't necessarily mean you can do. Rather than push yourself, think back to where you were when you started and how far you've progressed. Be patient.

WARMING UP/ NECK EXERCISES

HEAD ROTATION: This exercise should be performed slowly using a circular movement either left to right or right to left. Do ten times on each side.

1. **Starting position, looking straight ahead.**
2. **Start the head rotation to the left.**
3. **Move downward.**
4. **Go straight down until your chin touches your chest.**
5. **Keep going to the right.**

3

1

4

2

5

6

6. Return to the starting point.

HEAD FORWARD/BACKWARD (Do this ten times)

1. Hold head straight and look forward.
2. Go forward as far as possible. Your chin should be up against your chest.
3. Slowly go back.
4. Take it slowly back all the way.

▼

1

3

2

4

1

3

2

4

▲

HEAD SIDE-TO-SIDE (Do this ten times)

1. Hold head straight and look forward.
2. Slowly tilt the head to the right in a relaxed manner.
3. Return to the center.
4. Slowly tilt the head to the left in a relaxed manner.

WRIST EXERCISES ▶

WRIST STRETCH (Do ten times on each side)

1. Extend right arm and turn outward. Left hand is in a grab position.

1

2. Left hand grabs the right hand. Left palm is on top of right back hand.
3. Start bringing the wrist toward your chest (keep elbow up).

2

3

WRIST STRETCH II (Do ten times on each side)

1. Right palm faces up. Left hand is under right.
2. Left thumb is on back of right hand. The left fingers grab palm and thumb of right hand.
3. Start pushing with left thumb and pulling with left finger. Create a tension simultaneously going outward and downward.
4. Go down as far as possible

1

2

3

4

1

4

2

5

3

▲

ELBOW AND WRIST STRETCH (Do five times on each side)

1. Turn both arms outward and put left on top of right.
2. Have both palms facing each other.
3. Cross fingers and extend arms.
4. Start moving toward chest. Then go up and out to extend.
5. Slowly return to starting position.

SHOULDER EXERCISES

SHOULDER I (Perform ten-to-15 times at normal speed)

1. **Extend arms in front at shoulder level.**
2. **Twist in elbows and make fists.**
3. **Keep your elbows in and slide them on their sides.**
4. **Extend arms slowly, keeping elbows in.**
5. **Bring your arms back in front with**

3

1

4

2

5

1

SHOULDER ROTATION (Should be done ten times both forward and backward)

1. From the starting position.
2. Shoulders go forward.
3. Shoulders go up.
4. Shoulders go all the way back.
5. Shoulders go halfway down and come

4

2

5

3

ARM ROTATIONS (Keep your arms fully extended, feet a shoulder-width apart. Do 20 times)

1. Extend your arms in front.

1

2

5

2. Start a downward rotation.
3. Keep the rotation going in back.
4. Keep the rotation going in front.
5. Rotate straight up.
6. Then forward.
7. Return to starting point.

3

6

4

7

1

3

2

4

ISOMETRIC PRESSURE EXERCISES

NECK (Use your hands to hold pressure for five seconds)

1. Stand with the right hand in front of your face.
2. Place your right hand in front. Slowly push your head back.
3. Start pressure with your hand while your head tilts forward.
4. Maintaining pressure, keep head going as far as possible.

1

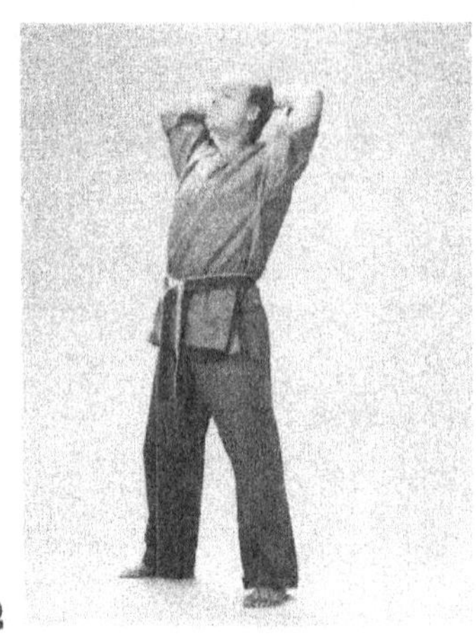

2

NECK (Both hands are behind neck, tilt back)

1. Stand with your hands behind your head. Tilt forward and relax.
2. Start pressure on the back of the head. Move head backward.
3. Maintaining pressure, take head all the way

3

1

NECK (Ono hand on one side of the head. Tilt sideways)

1. Stand with left hand on side of the head.
2. Slowly push head In the opposite direction. Relax.
3. Start the pressure as you tilt the head to one side.
4. Maintaining pressure, tilt the head all the

3

2

4

ARMS WITH PRESSURE

ARMS PRESSURE I
(Palms face the back of partner's hands. Two sets of each)

1. Standing with hands together, partner has hands on top of yours.
2. You start opening hands as partner offers resistance. Keep trying to open your hands as partner gradually gives you opening.
3. Keep going until hands are three feet apart.

1

1

2

2

ARMS PRESSURE II
(Palms facing each other. Two sets of each)

1. Standing and facing partner, your left hand Is at shoulder level facing down and your right hand Is at abs level facing up. Partner Is doing opposite.
2. Make contact with partner and begin pressure on each other's palms.
3. Keep pressure high to head level and low to belt level. Keep control

3

3

1

REVERSE ARMS PRESSURE II

1. Standing and facing partner, your right hand la at shoulder level facing down and your left hand is at abs level facing up.
2. Make contact with your partner and begin pressure on each other's palms.
3. Keep pressure high to head level and low to belt level. Keep control as you gradually release.

1

2

2

3

ARMS PRESSURE I REVERSE

(Palms facing back of partner's hands)

1. Stand facing partner. Start opening hands as he gives resistance.
2. Keep opening hands as partner gradually surrenders.
3. Keep going until palms are three feet apart.

1

4

2

5

3

ANKLES STRETCH (Rotate forward and backward. Do ten times. Also, make a circle forward and backward. Do it left and right ten times.)

1. Sit with right leg on top of left.
2. Grab foot.
3. Pull back foot.
4. Do movement going up.
5. Keep going forward.

6

6. Return to starting point.

CALF STRETCH (Do ten times, holding each position for three seconds)

1. Sit relaxed, leg extended.
2. Bring back feet and toes without touching floor.
3. Return to starting position.
4. Point feet and toes forward.

▼

1

3

2

4

STANDING KNEE ROTATION (Perform full circle, do ten times)

1. Bend forward, hands on knees.
2. Slowly move to left in a circular motion.
3. Keep going on the other side and return to starting point.

◄

1

2 2

STANDING I (Two times on each leg)

1. Standing on right leg, lift left knee.
2. Grab knee and shin.
3. Pull back to chest, hold ten seconds.

►

3 3

STANDING CALF STRETCH (Stand with hands against wall)

1. Left leg in front and close to wall. Right leg is back.
2. Fully extend right leg and hold for ten seconds. Do two sets using both right and left legs.

◄

2

3

1

SQUATTING (Do two sets ten times)

1. Stand with the legs wide, hands on waist.
2. Start going down.
3. Keep going down, with back straight.
4. Assume a comfortable and proper low stance and return to starting position.

►

4

DEEP FRONT STANCE (Two sot* of ten reps; hold each rep two seconds)

1. Stand with left leg in front, both legs straight.
2. Start getting into front stance.
3. Keep going lower.
4. Go to your maximum and hold for two seconds. Then bounce back and go again.

1

2

3

4

DEEP BACK STANCE (Two sots of ten reps; hold each rep two seconds)

1. High back stance.
2. Slowly go backward.
3. As you go back toes are up, heels on floor. Hold, then back slowly to start.

1

2

3

JUMPING (Two sets of 20)

1. Stand ready.
2. Jump.
3. Legs land wide open, hands touch each other.

1

2

3

. **CHAPTER 3**

Superstretching Exercises

you've mastered all the stretching exercises in my first book, you are ready for the ultimate in flexibility programs. My superstretching routine is not for the beginner or even intermediate student; it's for the martial artist who is ready to reach new heights and discover new limits. This program goes beyond anything you thought possible.

How do you know you're ready? If you practiced and mastered all the exercises in the first book for at least six months, feel comfortable with the new limits you've created and can either do the splits or come within a few inches of the floor, then you're ready for the most exciting stretching regimen in existence today.

I've received many letters from people wondering why I created a superstretching level. Everybody has a goal, some to the point of obsession. One person even wrote and asked me if having a ligament surgically removed would help him do the splits. There are easier ways, I wrote back, such as my superstretching program.

I'm not like the everyday person out there. I'm one of the few who can get up in the morning and immediately do the splits. But I won't without first warming up. Although I am very flexible, I will not try anything difficult until the basic stretching exercises have been completed.

Admittedly, there are times when I would just as soon skip the stretching routine and go right to my serious martial arts work. But if you don't train, you lose your ability very quickly. While I'm flexible, if I stopped stretching and training for three months I'd surrender a great deal of my overall flexibility. Twenty-to-30 minutes per day is but a small price to pay considering the risks involved. By becoming lazy or less diligent in my training, I chance suffering a serious injury which could put me on the sidelines indefinitely.

SUPERSTRETCHING

ROLL-ON SPLITS (Do ten times)

1. Sitting in full split.
2. Roll forward with chest on floor.
3. Push back and start rolling, bringing back legs.
4. Roll on your back with legs straight up.
5. Grab from inside and open.
6. Hold your head up and keep opening.

1

4

2

5

3

6

7. Open as far as possible.
8. Start bringing back legs up.
9. Keep bringing legs forward.

10. Open as far as possible. Legs are in synch with landing.
11. Keep going forward.
12. Roll forward as far as possible.

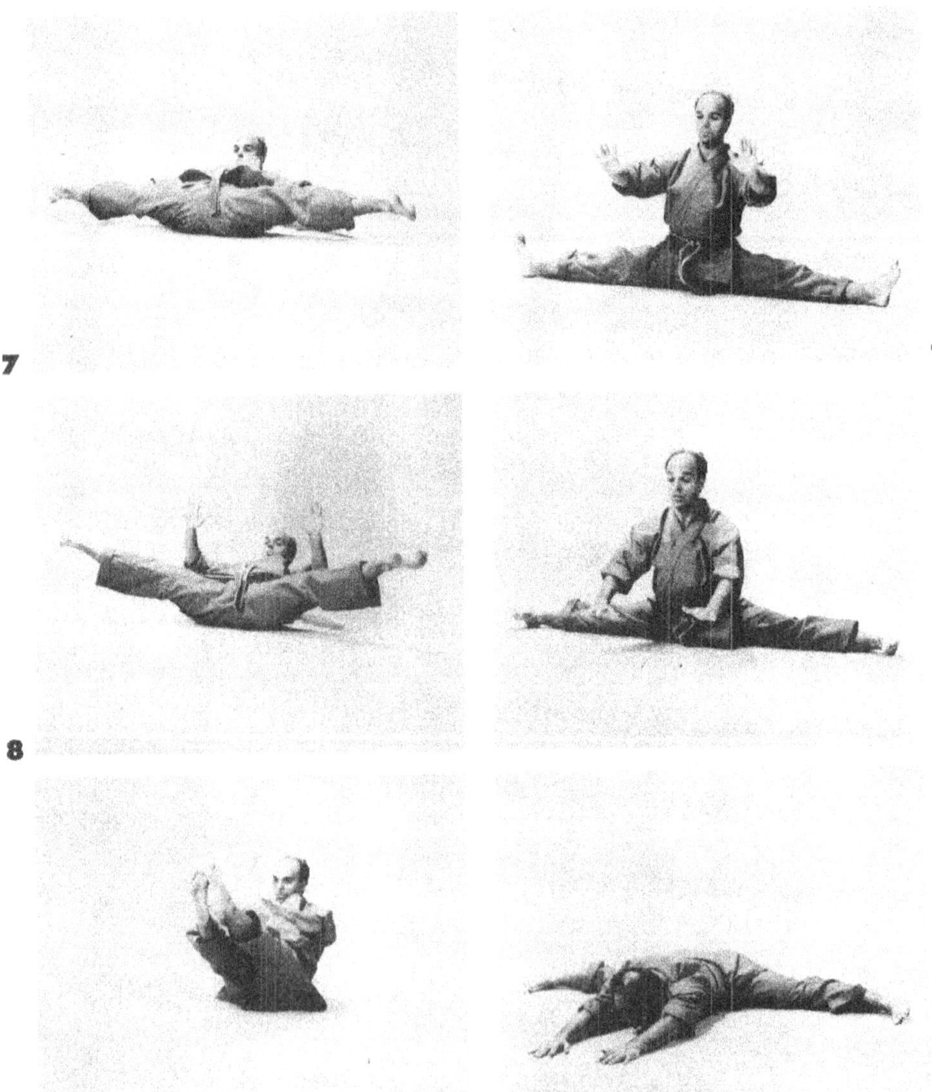

7 10

8 11

9 12

1

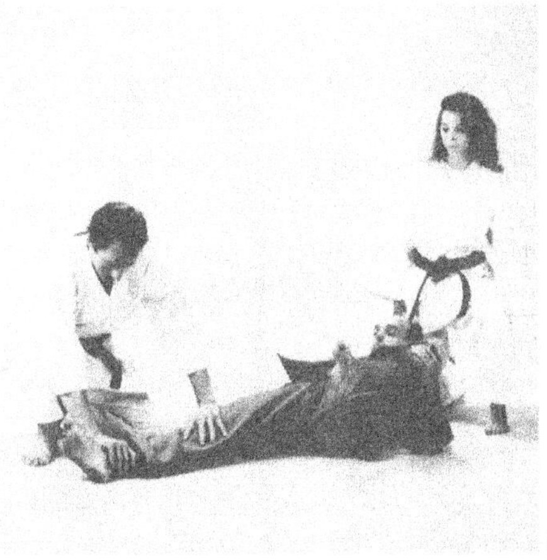

3

2

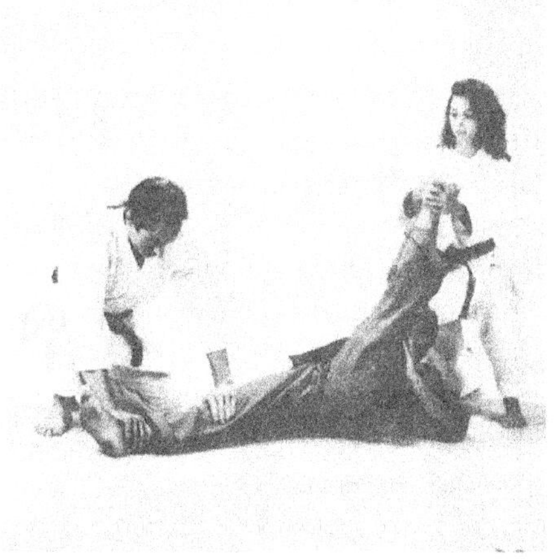

4

3-PARTNER STRETCH (Room of torture)

1. Three people on floor.
2. Partner A grabs your right leg at the ankle.
3. Lift your knee.
4. Partner B grabs your extended left leg.
5. The second partner starts to stretch your leg by pulling down.

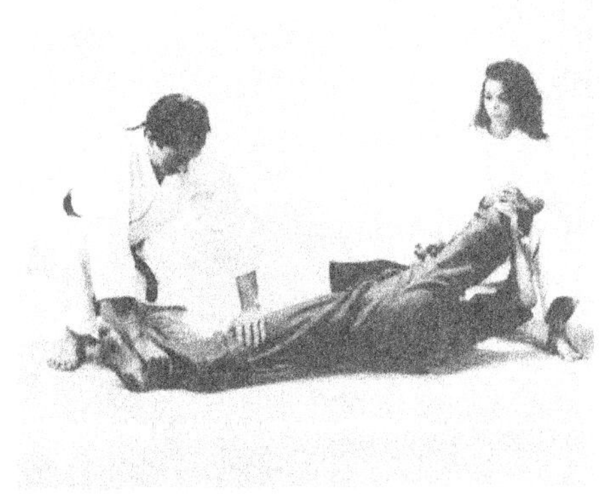

5

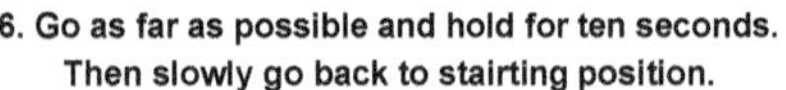
6. Go as far as possible and hold for ten seconds. Then slowly go back to stairting position.

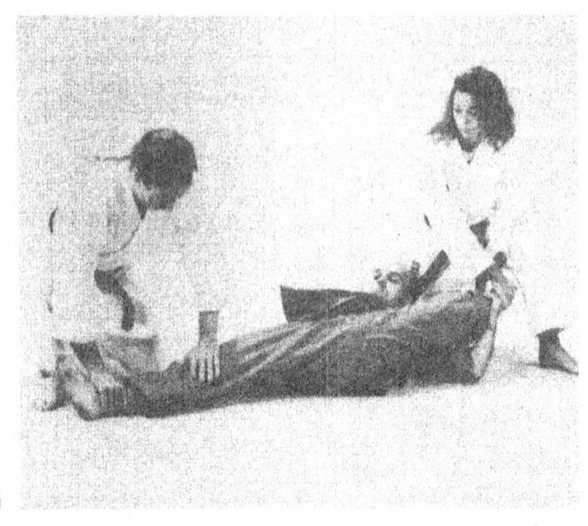
6

ROOM OF TORTURE

1. Three people on floor.
2. Open legs as each partner grabs one of your ankles.
3. Slowly go down.
4. Go as far as possible and hold for ten seconds. Relax and breathe easy.

▼

1

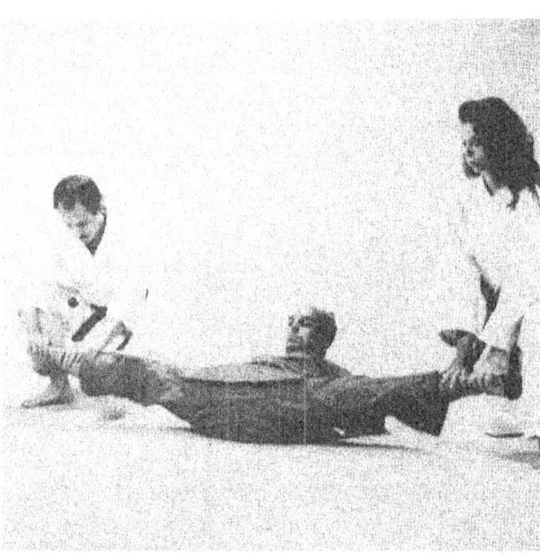
3

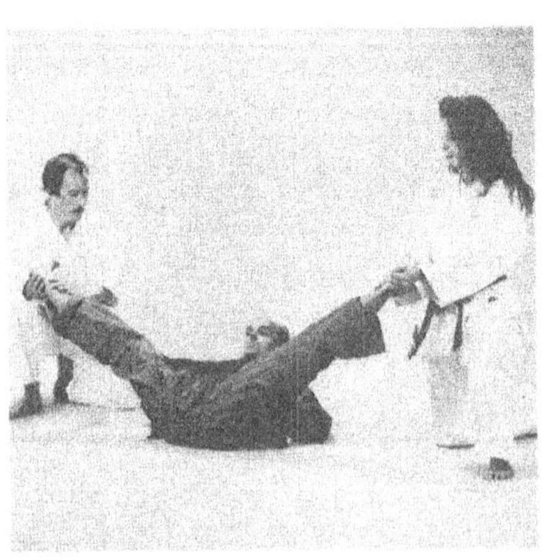
2

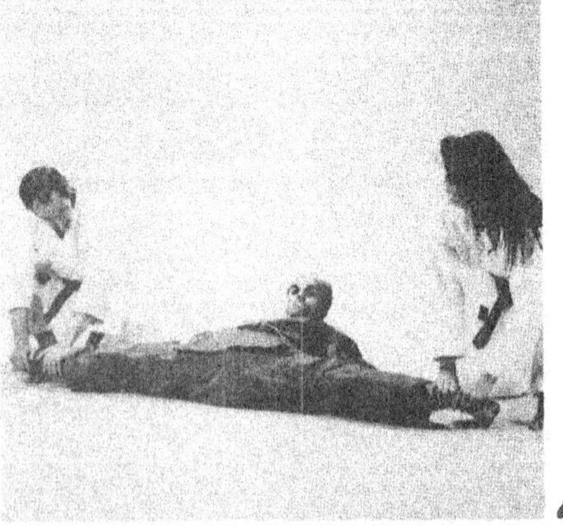
4

3 PARTNER STRETCH I (One partner holds your hand and upper body while the other lifts your knee and holds belt)

1. As you're standing, partner A holds your belt and hand.
2. Partner B slowly lifts your knee.
3. Go as far as you can and hold for ten seconds. Partner A should keep your upper body straight.

1

2

3

3-PARTNER STRETCH II (Do left to right)

1. Stand with partners.

1

2

4

2. Bend forward toward your left leg.
3. Lift right leg up and bring your chest to your left leg.
4. Go as far as possible with your partners pushing. Hold your head to your shin for ten seconds.

3

3-PARTNER STRETCH III (Partner A must push on your hips and forearms; partner B must lift as much as possible)

1. Stand with partners, with partner A holding your hand and belt.

▼

1

2. Lift leg as though doing a side kick. Keep a straight line with the upper body.
3. Keep going up.
4. Go as far as you can and hold for ten seconds.
5. Partner A should grab your belt.

4-PARTNER STRETCH (The partner under you must be stable)

1. Stand with two partners, with the third kneeling.
2. Put your back against your partner's back.
3. Extend your right leg.
4. Extend your left leg in the opposite direction.

1

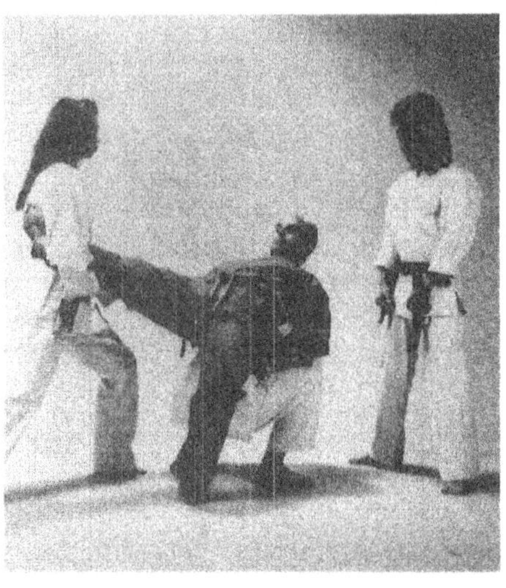

3

2

4

5

5. Stretch as far as you can. The partner under you will slowly move up. Do this for ten seconds.

4-PARTNER STRETCH II

1. Get in position.
2. Your back again is against your partner's back.

1

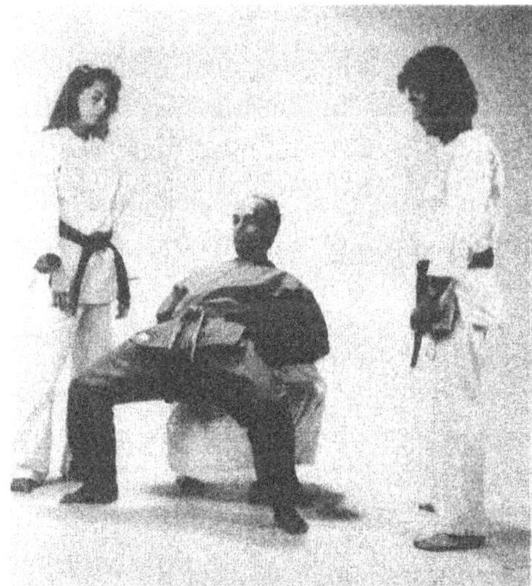

2

3. Lift your right leg sideways.
4. Lift your left leg sideways.

5. Start stretching as your partner underneath begins to rise.
6. Go as far as possible and hold for ten seconds.

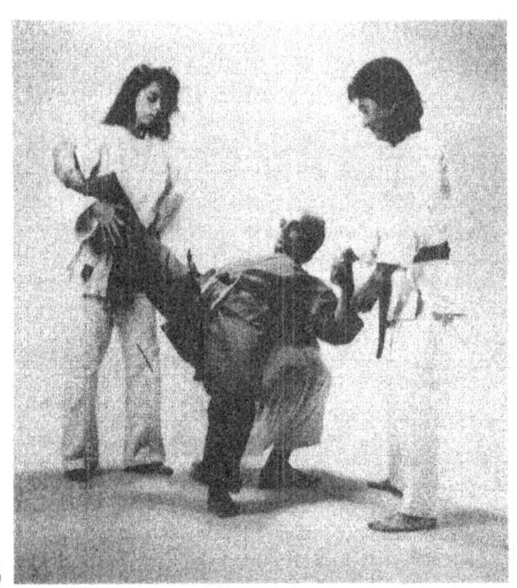
3

5

4

6

ᒥNER STRETCH IV (Mid-air splits)

1. Stand with partners.
2. Your partners hold your right side kick.
3. Your partners hold your left side kick. Use partners' shoulders for balance.
4. Let yourself go down into a splits position.

1

3

2

4

5. Contract Inner thigh muscle and go up. You can use your arms to push.
6. Pivot 180 degrees to right and let yourself go down Into a splits position.
7. Contract inner thighs and go up.
8. Let yourself go down Into a full splits position.

5

7

6

8

: CHAPTER 4

Super Kicking and Jump Kicking Drills

ISUPER KICKING

Despite what you may have been led to believe, there is more to a kick than simply extending the leg. Much of what is accomplished in a tournament has been honed during stretching and flexibility training. When you are exercising, you should be aware of what your body is doing. You should know which muscle is involved in the exercise, know which muscles are strong or weak and which need the most work.

We spend time stretching not only to become more flexible and comfortable, but also to give our stances and forms stability and control. And so as we are performing our daily stretching routines, we must remember that what we do in those daily 20-to- 30-minute exercises will be put into practice on the competition floor.

Lack of flexibility, which is the byproduct of an inadequate stretching routine, will manifest itself in poor balance, improper focus and control, sagging posture, and diminishing power and execution. Without this foundation training, the kick and punch you have worked long to master will be missing the main ingredients—weak pivot foot, an upper body that is out of control, and arms that hamper rather than help in the execution of the technique.

STRONG SUPPORTING LEG

A lot of people attempt kicks, but they don't know how to pivot on the supporting leg. Since the supporting leg always is in a bad position, the ankle shifts in and out. These mistakes may fool your training partner in class, but they won't get past the keen eyes of the judges.

UPPER BODY POSITION

Also important is the weight position of the upper body. If your weight is too much inside, outside or backward, you'll lose your balance and fall when you throw a kick. You must adjust the weight of your upper body so that it rests directly on top of the

balancing foot. This way, the weight of the kick is going forward and the technique will be applied with power and focus.

ARM POSITION

Another point to be considered is the position of the arms. When most people kick they allow their arms to fly in different directions. This not only detracts from the look of the form, it also reduces the strength and momentum of the technique. All the movement of a form must be traveling the same way; otherwise, you're fighting against yourself and the form suffers.

I'm sure you've seen plenty of performers who have flashy kicks in their repertoire. However, when it comes time forthem to display power, they fall horribly short. It's great to be flexible and have a nice-looking kick, but, unless there is some punch behind the movement, it's a wasted technique. Some instructors believe the moreflexibleyouare, the less power you have. That's true if you only work on stretching and not strengthening. The rubber-band approach to kicking—being high and flexible, but without explosive power—only looks good until it must be used in application.

One way to build kicking power is through the strenuous partner stretching exercises. When the partner(s) moves back, increase your resistence as you try to maintain your balance.

JUMP KICKING DRILLS

There are three fundamental components to a basic jump kick—the jump and kick itself, and the power-extension combination created by a perfectly executed kick. If you fail in one of those three areas, you're technique becomes a series of unrelated movements.

The allure of a jump kick is not merely to see how high you can get, although it is one of the main drawing points if you judge solely by crowd reaction. It's also how you get there and what you do once you reach the top that separates the champions from the also-rans.

The key word is control—during takeoff, application of technique and eventual landing. Once you have reached the desired height, you must show that your kick has strength, extension, power and focus. More than just pushing the leg out to the side, a jump kick should be a solid, controlled extension of your body.

SUPERKICKING

BASIC KICK—Front kick (Lift knee, pivot on supporting leg, balance your weight on top of supporting leg, and hold hand position)

1. Assume stance.
2. Lift knee and pivot on supporting foot.
3. Extend and kick, showing good balance and stance.
4. Chamber with balance.
5. Go back to starting stance.

3

1

4

2

5

SIDE KICK

1. Assume stance.
2. Lift up knee, a bit inside. Rear foot is ready to strike. Pivot on supporting leg.
3. Extend the leg, using a forward hip motion.
4. Chamber with balance.
5. Return to stance.

3

1

4

2

5

ROUND KICK (Circular movement from back leg)

1. Assume stance.
2. Lift knee from side in circular motion and keep going in circular movement until in front of target. Pivot on supporting foot.
3. Extend fully.
4. Return to original position.
5. Back into original stance.

3

1

4

2

5

HOOK KICK

1. Assume stance.
2. Lift knee a bit to the outside.
3. Extend the leg.
4. Start circular movement.
5. Hook.

6

7

▲

6. Chamber.
7. Return to original stance.

1

◀

SPIN HOOK

1. Assume stance.
2. Start spin, pivoting inward and using arms.
3. Looking forward, pivot 360 degrees.

2

3

4. Lift knee.
5. Extend.
6. Circular motion.

7. Hook.
8. Maintain circular motion.
9. Return to original stance (you have completed a full circle).

SPIN BACK

1. Assume stance.
2. Start spin, pivoting inward and using arms.
3. Looking forward, pivot 360 degrees.
4. Lift knee, with heel ready to strike.
5. Start extension with heel first.

3

1

4

2

5

6

8

7

9

6. Full extension.
7. Chamber with balance.
8. Pivot back, facing target.
9. Return to original stance.

1

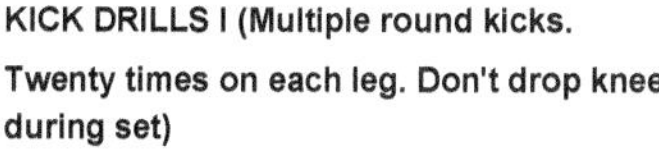

KICK DRILLS I (Multiple round kicks.

Twenty times on each leg. Don't drop knee during set)

1. Standing

2

2. Lift knee.
3. Start extension.
4. Full extension.
5. Bring back.
6. Kick again.

5

6

3

4

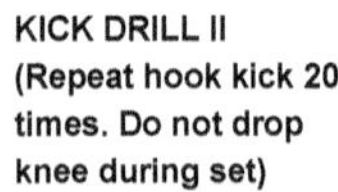

KICK DRILL II
(Repeat hook kick 20 times. Do not drop knee during set)

1. Stand, left leg in front

1

2

5

3

6

4

2. Chamber knee sideways.
3. Extend leg inside, with heel out.
4. Start circular motion.
5. Hook kick.
6. Chamber.

KICK DRILL III (Repeat round kick, hook kick combination. Do ten times with each leg. Do not drop knee)

1. Stand, left leg in front.
2. Chamber knee in center.
3. Extend for round kick.
4. Deliver round kick at head level.
5. Chamber.

3

4

5

1

2

6. Bring knee inside.
7. Extend inside at head level.
8. Start circular motion.
9. Hook kick.
10. Hook full.
11. Chamber.

1

4

2

5

3

SLOW KICK TEST (Slowly perform hook kick from both far and In close so you must go higher. Perform every movement slowly. This exercise helps you with balance, strength, focus, and technique)

1. Stand six feet from partner, feet together.
2. Chamber knee.
3. Extend leg left inside.
4. Hook kick to abs level.
5. Place left foot closer to partner.

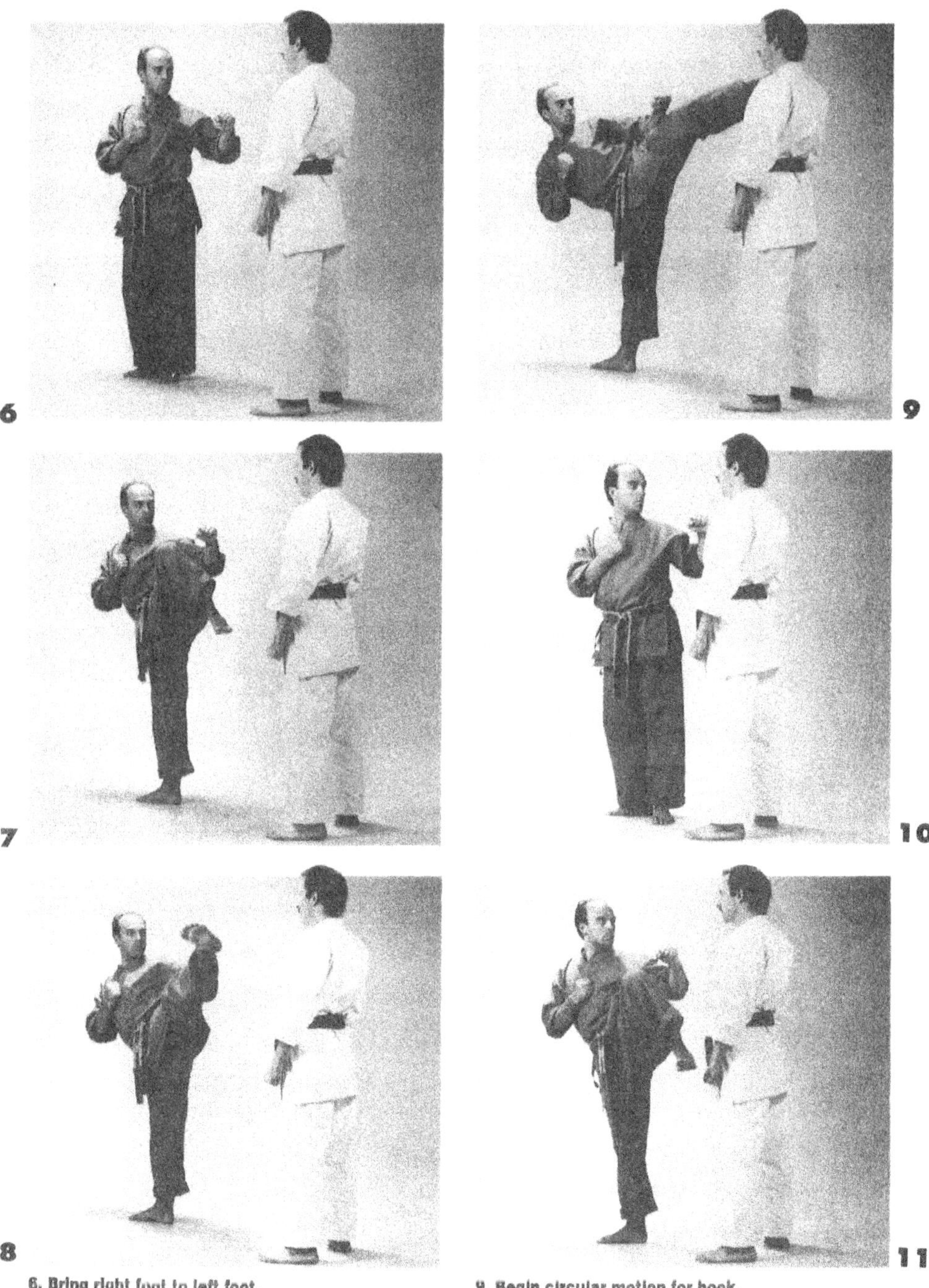

6. Bring right foot to left foot.
7. Chamber.
8. Extend leg.

9. Begin circular motion for hook.
10. Place left foot closer to partner.
11. Chamber.

12

14

13

15

12. Extend leg.
13. Perform circular motion for hook kick.
14. Hook kick and chamber.
15. Place left foot closer to partner.

SLOW KICK COMBINATION (Perform slow kick drills extremely slow. Do at least five times with each leg. This example is among unlimited possibilities)

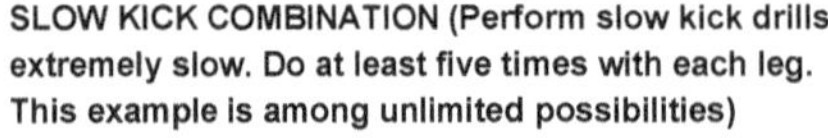

1. Assume left front stance in front of partner.

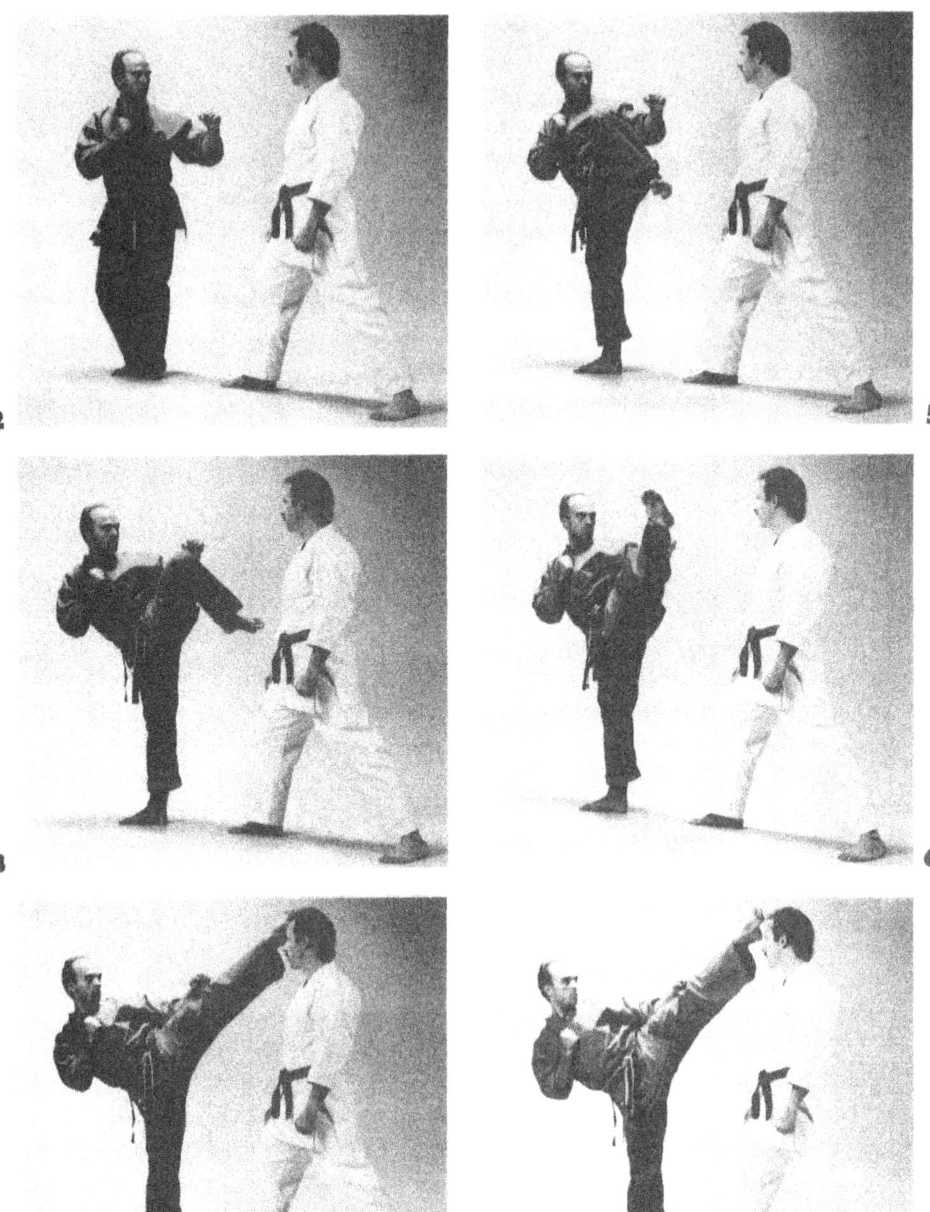

2. Bring right leg forward to left leg (sliding slowly).
3. Chamber for round kick.
4. Extend round kick to head.

5. Start hook motion.
6. Begin hook kick.
7. Chamber for side kick.

8

11

9

12

10

13

8. Hook full.
9. Chamber for side kick.
10. Extend side kick to head.

11. Chamber.
12. Bring back left leg to start.
13. Slide back right leg to start position.

1

KICKING COMBINATION

COMBINATION I

1. Front stance right.
2. Chamber left knee.
3. Round kick high left.
4. Chamber.
5. Side kick high left.
6. Chamber.

4

2

5

3

6

7

7. High side kick.
8. Move forward in left back stance.

8

1

COMBINATION II

1. Assume back stance, left leg in front.
2. Bring right leg to left foot.
3. Chamber left knee.

2

3

4

5. Chamber.
6. Low side kick.
7. Chamber.
8. Extend high to the right.
9. Start hook kick.
10. Perform full hook kick.

5

8

6

9

7

10

11

11. Chamber.
12. Round kick high.
13. Chamber.
14. Fall forward left into back stance.

12

13

14

(48) COMBINATION III

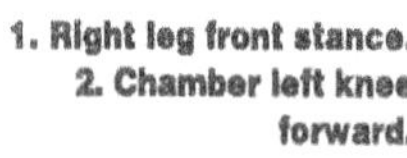

1. Right leg front stance.
2. Chamber left knee forward.

1

2

3. High front kick.
4. Chamber on side at 45 degrees.
5. Low side kick at 45 degrees.
6. Chamber.
7. High side kick at 45 degrees.
8. Chamber.

3

4

5

6

7

8

9

◄

9. Land 45 degrees into back stance. Left leg in front.

3

COMBINATION IV

1. Right leg front stance.
2. Chamber left knee.
3. Round kick 45 degrees to right.
4. Chamber.
5. Low side kick 45 degrees to left.

1

4

2

5

6

6. Chamber.
7. Low round kick right 45 degrees.
8. Chamber.
9. High side kick 45 degrees to left.
10. Chamber.
11. Extend 45 degrees to right.

9

7

10

8

11

12

12. Start circular motion.
13. Hook kick in center.
14. Round kick in center.
15. Chamber.

13

14

15

COMBINATION V (Keep balance, turn head first)

1. Right front stance.
2. Start spinning.

1

2

3

3. Spin 360 degrees.
4. Chamber left leg.
5. Extend.
6. Start hook kick and follow through on the hook kick.
7. Spin another 180 degrees.
8. Chamber.

6

4

7

5

8

9

9. Side kick high.
10. Land in a left leg front stance.

10

COMBINATION VI

1. Right leg front stance.
2. Chamber left leg in front.
3. Front kick at head level.
4. Chamber.

1

2

3

4

5

5. Pivot inside in the opposite direction.
6. Chamber left knee.
7. Left round kick high.
8. Chamber.
9. Return to first position, pivoting 180 degrees.

8

6

9

7

COMBINATION VII
(Practice balance and control)

1. Right leg front stance.

▶

1

2. Chamber left leg •ideway*.
3. Side kick, head level.
4. Chamber.
5. Pivot inside in the opposite direction. 6. Left knee and chamber sideways.
7. High side kick.

2

5

3

6

4

7

8

8. Fall forward into back stance.
9. Left leg in front.

9

1

COMBINATION VIII

1. Right leg front stance.
2. Slide back or left leg to front or right leg.
3. Chamber right knee to the front.

2

3

4

5

5. Chamber.
6. Bring back foot to left foot.
7. Chamber left knee 180 degrees in opposite direction.
8. Side kick high.
9. Chamber.
10. Pivot inside 180 degrees.

8

6

9

7

10

11

12

11. Chamber left knee to the front.

12. Front kick high.

13. Chamber.

14. Land forward into left

13

14

JUMP KICKS

JUMP FRONT KICK

1. Left leg front stance. 2. Push with the left leg and bring up right knee.

1

2

3

3. Switch. Bring up left knee and control in mid-air.

4. Start front kick.

5. Front kick, fully extended.

6. Land on right foot first.

7. Land into left front

4

6

5

7

1

2

3

4

JUMP SIDE KICK

1. Right leg front stance.
2. Push with right leg to get airborne. Bring left knee up sideways.
3. Tuck right leg, control in mid-air.
4. Perform side kick with left leg.

5

5. Chamber left leg, extend right leg under.
6. Land on right foot.
7. Land into left front stance.

6

7

1

JUMP ROUND KICK

1. Left leg front stance.

2

2. Push with left leg, bring right knee up.

3

3. Bring left knee up in circular motion.
4. Round kick in mid-air.
5. Chamber left leg, extend right leg under.
6. Land on right foot.
7. Land in left front stance.

4 6 5 7

1

3

2

JUMP SPIN HOOK

1. Right leg front stance.
2. Start spinning, keeping eye contact.
3. Chamber left knee, lock right and Jump spin.
4. Extend left leg for hook kick.

4

5

5. Hook kick in mid-air.
6. Land on right foot.
7. Finish circular motion, then land in front stance.

6

7

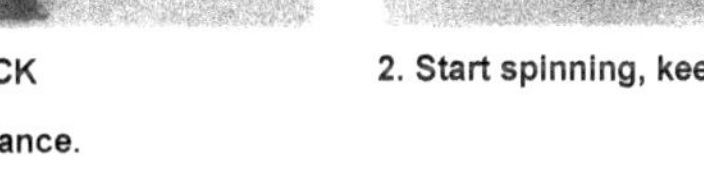

JUMP SPIN BACK KICK

1. Right leg front stance.

2. Start spinning, keeping eye contact.

3

3. Keep spinning, pivot feet.
4. Jump, chamber left knee, tuck right under.
5. Perform back kick, control in mid-air.
6. Land on right leg, chamber left.
7. Land forward in left leg front stance.

4

6

5

7

1

2

3

KICKING IMPACT (Power)

FRONT KICK

1. Stand with partner holding shield.
2. Begin with the left knee in direction of impact.
3. Impact. Use hip movement to help penetration.

SIDE KICK

1. Stand with partner holding shield.
2. Bring back leg to front leg. Maintain hand position.
3. Chamber knee, with foot position left.

▼

1

2

3

4

4. Impact using hip movement.

1

2

ROUND KICK

1. Stand with partner holding shield.
2. Lift knee from back leg in a circular direction.
3. Pivot on the supporting leg and impact.

HOOK KICK

1. Stand with partner holding focus pad.
2. Chamber left leg.

1

2

3

3

5

4

6

3. Extend leg.
4. Perform hook movement with leg.
5. Follow through.
6. Land in stance.

SPIN HOOK

1. Stand with partner holding two focus pads at head level, a shoulder-width apart.
2. Start spinning.

1

2

3

5

4

6

3. Chamber knee.
4. Extend left.

5. Perform hook movement.

SPIN BACK

1. Stand with partner holding shield.

2. Start spinning.

1

2

3

4

5

▲

3. Perform second half of spinning movement.
4. Chamber knee.
5. Impact with heel.

JUMP FRONT KICK

1. Stand with partner holding focus pad at head level or higher.
2. Take off, lifting right knee.

▼

1

2

JUMP SIDE KICK

1. Stand with partner holding shield.
2. Take off, lifting left knee.
3. Tuck right leg, showing control in mid-air.

▼

1

2

3

3

4

5

▲

3. Shift, lifting left knee.
4. Start extension.
5. Kick for impact.

4

4. Kick for impact.

JUMP SPIN KICK

1. Start with partner holding focus pads.
2. Start spin motion.
3. Keep spinning, jump and chamber left knee.
4. Perform hook movement with leg.

1

3

2

4

1

2

JUMP SPIN BACK

1. Stand with partner holding shield.
2. Start spin motion.

3. Keep spinning, jump and chamber left knee.
4. Impact in mid-air.

CHAPTER 5

Weight Training For the Martial Artist

Weight training is nothing new to the martial arts. It's just that no one has ever considered the gym the right place to practice.

In ancient times, practitioners used the tools of the day or their weapons to build strength, power and endurance.Today, the philosophy remains the same, only the tools have changed to fit the need.

Remember: We're not trying to become body builders. We're not trying to build mass by using weights that are super heavy. Everything we do in the gym is geared toward being more explosive. Obviously, since we are lifting weights, increased mass and definition will be a byproduct. However, if you begin to look like Franco Columbo, then you're defeating the purpose of weightlifting.

SCHEDULE

Note: This program will help you build endurance and power. Use this program as a complement to your martial arts training.

Exercise	Sets	Repetitions
Bench Press	3	10
Dumbbell Press	3	10
Lat Pull Down (Behind Neck)	3	12
One-Hand Rowing (Two Sides)	3	12
Lateral Shoulders	2	18-20
Bent-Over Lateral Lat Shoulders	2	20
Triceps Push Down (Barbell)	4	20
Alternate Curl (With Dumbbell)	3	16
Leg Extension	3	25
Leg Curl	3	25
Calf Raises	3	25
Twist	1	5 Minutes

ABS

SITTING BENCH

1. Sitting on bench, lift knees up to chest level.
2. Extend both legs toward stomach level. Grab bench with both hands.
3. Bring back both knees together to starting point without dropping legs.

1

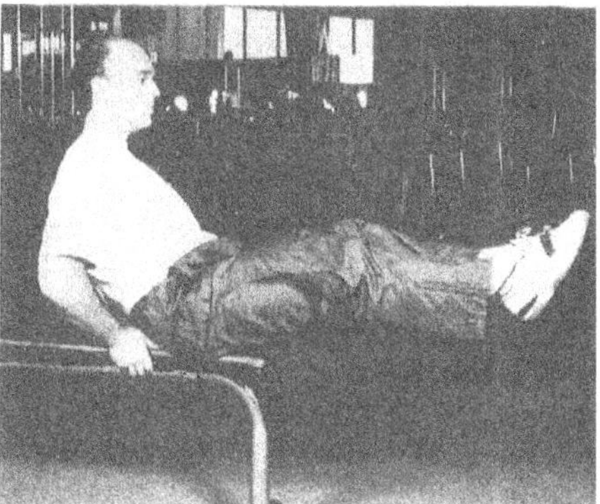

2

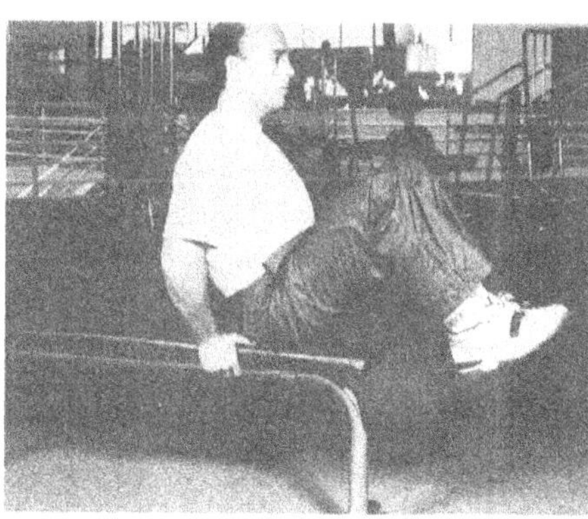

3

CRUNCHES

1. While on your back hold head up, with hands behind, knees up and create a 90-degree angle with feet.
2. Start to lift upper body toward knees.

▼

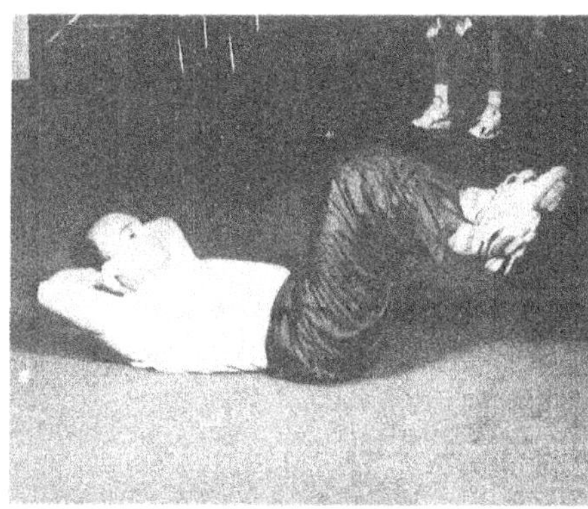

1

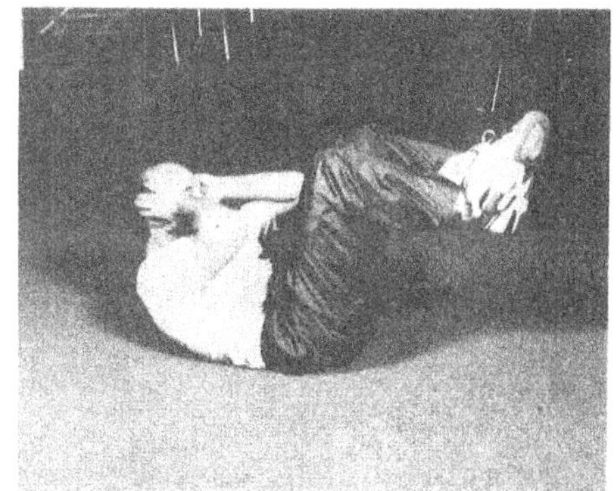

2

PUNCHING ABS (20 reps per set)

1. On your back with knees up, feet on floor. Hold your head up, fists on top of lower abs.
2. Lift upper body. Throw a left punch slowly in the center and hold for two seconds.
3. Slowly go back to starting point and keep the

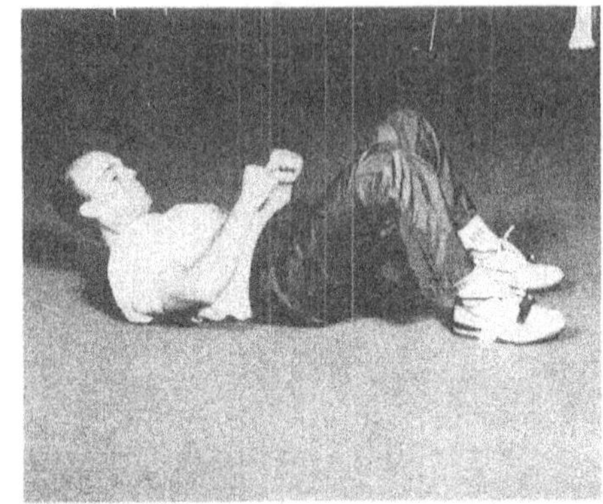

1

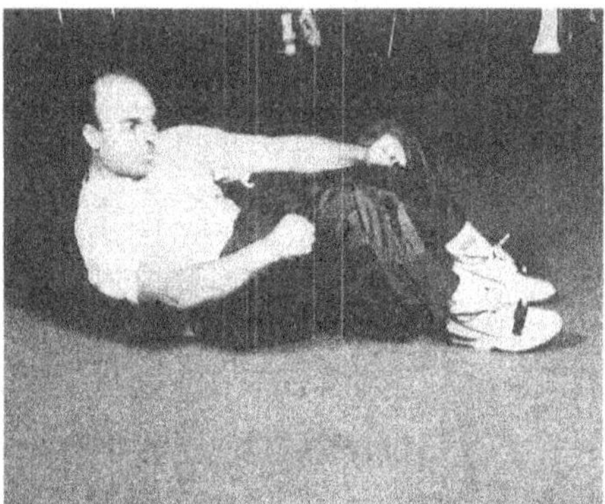

2

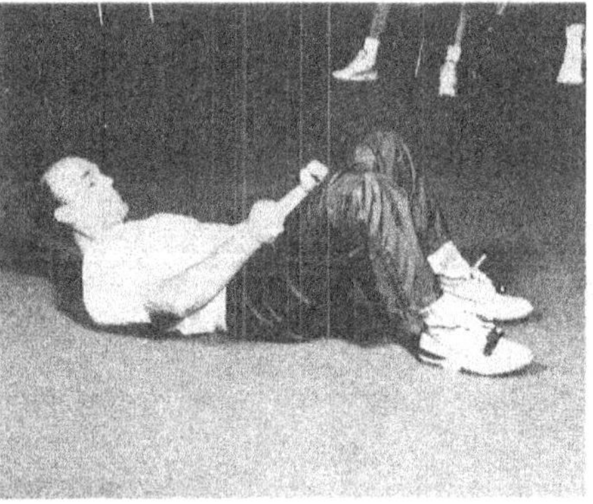

3

3. Make contact with the elbows and knees and hold it for one second.
4. Go back to starting point in control of movement.

▼

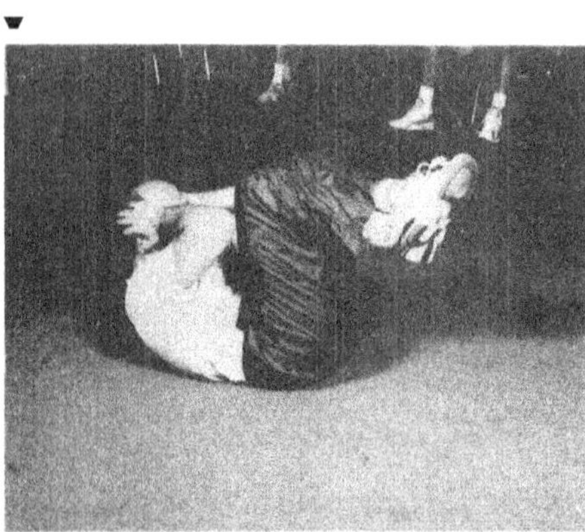

3

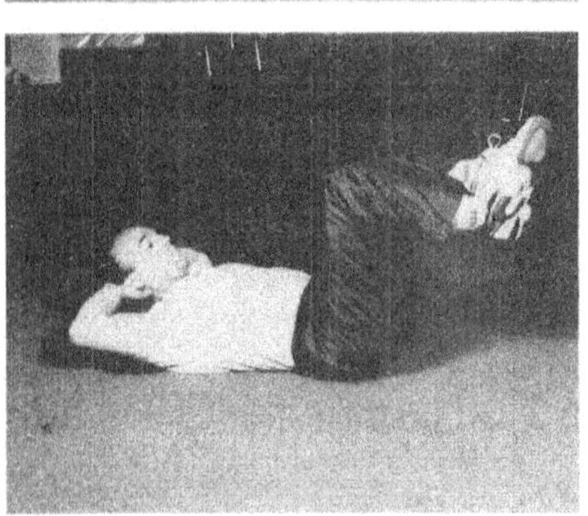

4

4

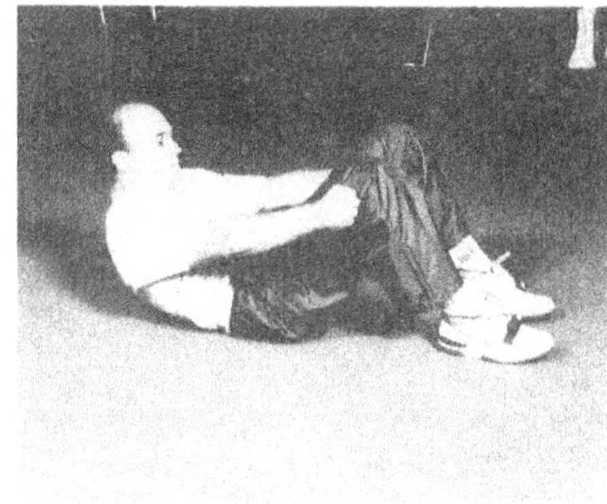

6

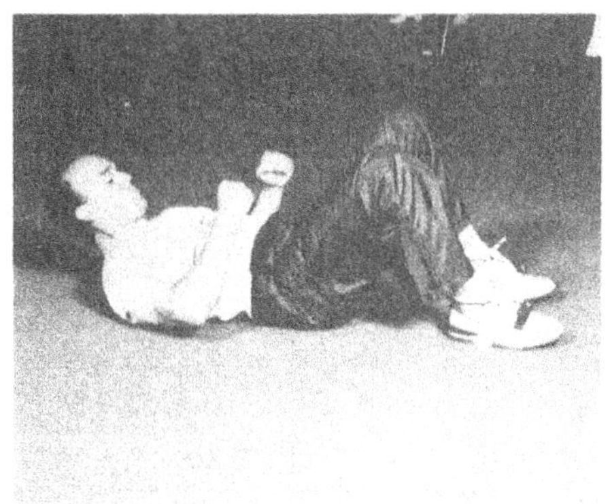

5

7

5. Lift upper body, throwing a right punch slowly in the center and hold it two seconds.
6. Slowly go back to starting point and keep the tension.

7. Lift upper body, throwing both left and right punches outside your knees and hold it for two seconds.
8. Go back to starting position.

1

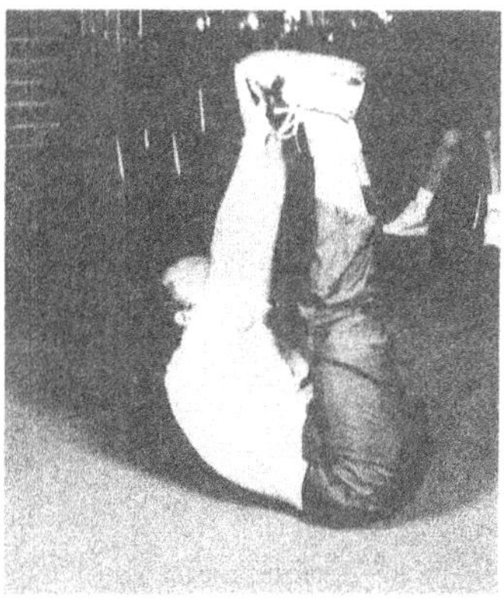

1. On your back, legs together and straight up at a 90-degree angle. Hold head up.

2. Contact abs, so touch toes and hold for one second. Do not move legs or feet.

3   4

Photos 3 and 4 are the same as 1 and 2.

WEIGHT TRAINING

BENCH PRESS/FLAT BENCH

1. Place grip on bar a few inches wider than the shoulder.
2. Go down with control, bring bar one inch from chest.
3. Push straight up. Repeat.

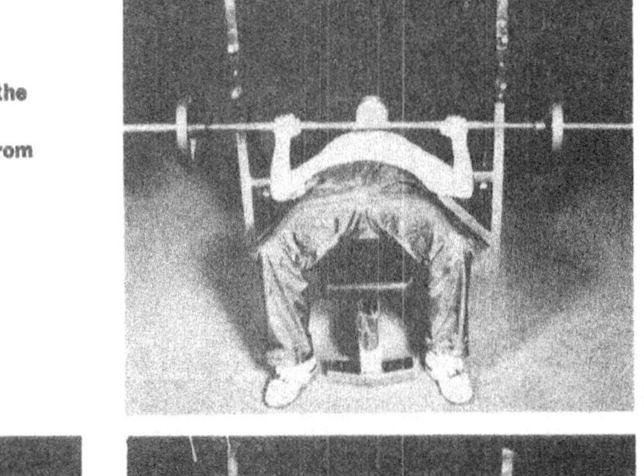

2

1   3

DUMBBELL PRESSES/INCLINE BENCH

1. Hold dumbbells up straight to the chest. Palm hands facing each other.
2. Open arms or elbows out at 90-degree angles with arms slowly going down.
3. Go down to maximum.
4. Push up with power and be explosive.
5. Finish movement, twisting inward and contracting

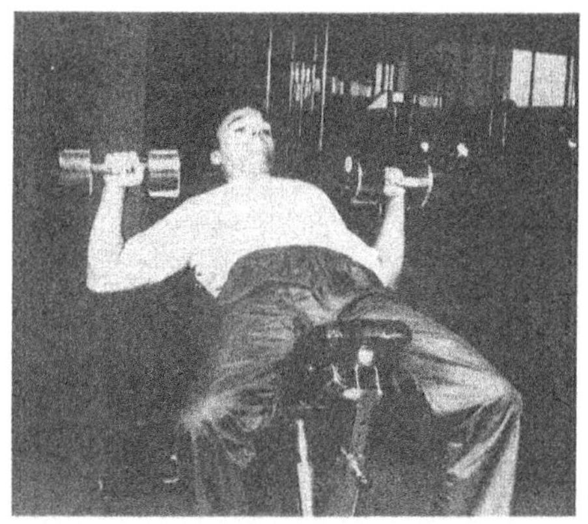
3

1

4

2

5

SHOULDER OR BEND-OVER LATERAL RAISE

1. Sitting feet together bend forward, hold dumbbell behind legs.
2. Raise side hands with control.
3. Go to maximum upward.
4. Slowly with control go back down.

1

2

3

4

5

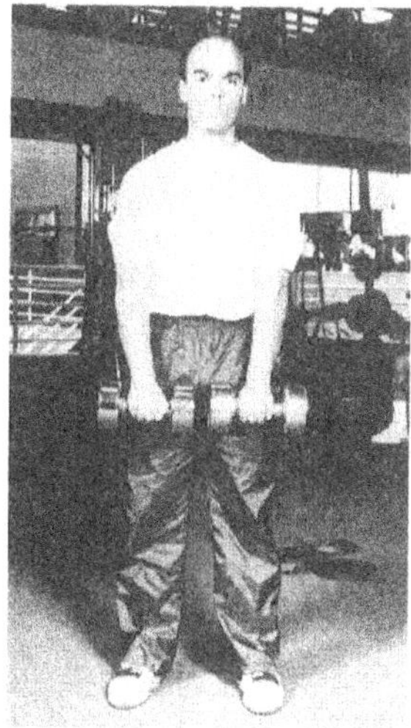

1

BICEPS SUPINATED CURLS/
DUMBBELLS

1. Stand with both hands in front, palms facing thighs.
2. Lift hand and turn inward.
3. Lift up to maximum, turning outward to straight line. Palm facing chest.
4. Go down, turning inward with control. Keep elbows in.
5. Return to starting position with control.

3

2

5

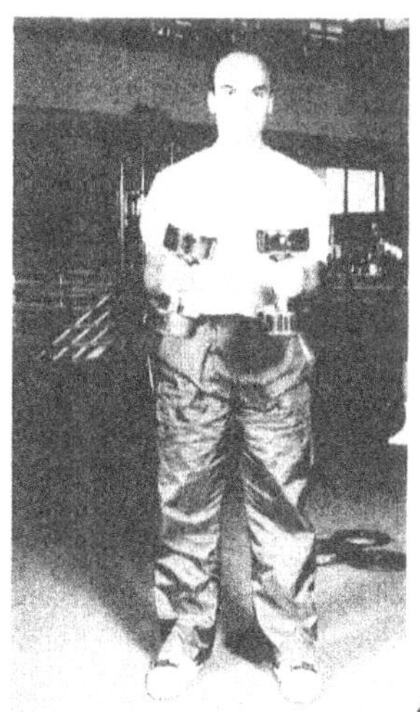

4

TRICEPS-PUSH DOWN (CABLE)

1. Grab handle tight. Keep elbow* at chest level.
2. Push straight down (concentrate on triceps) and be explosive.
3. Return slowly to starting

1

2

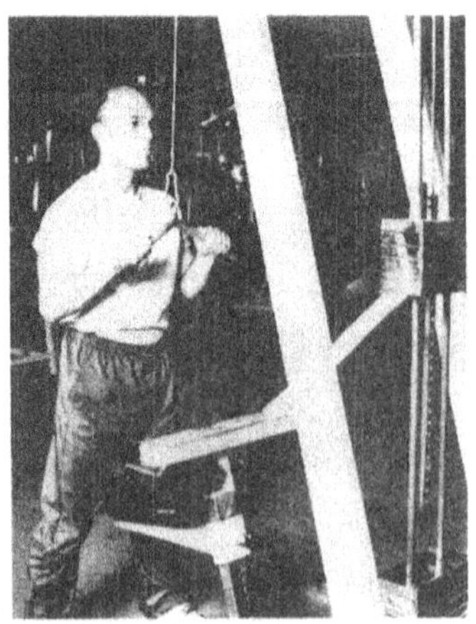

3

BACK PULL DOWN/CABLE

1. Sit, grab bar (after curve of the bar). Keep back straight. Pull down behind neck.
2. Hold it for one second.
3. Return slowly to starting

1

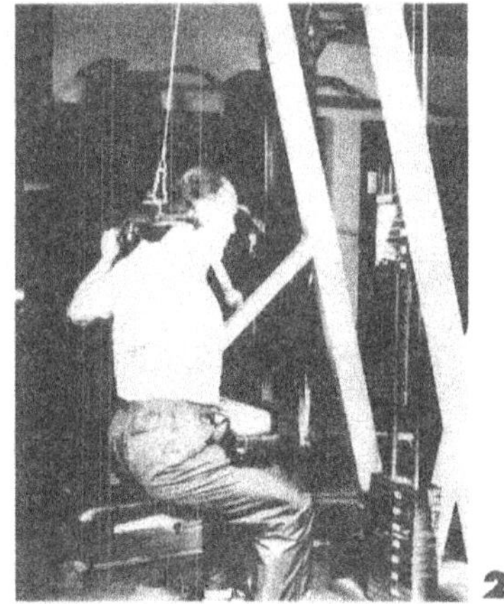

2

3

SHOULDER OR LATERAL RAISE DUMBBELL

1. Standing up, hold dumbbell in front.
2. Raise arm to the sides with a little turn up of the elbows. Hold it for one second.
3. Return slowly to starting

1

2

3

LEG/LEG EXTENSION

1. Sit in ready position.
2. Extension and hold for one second.
3. Return to start with

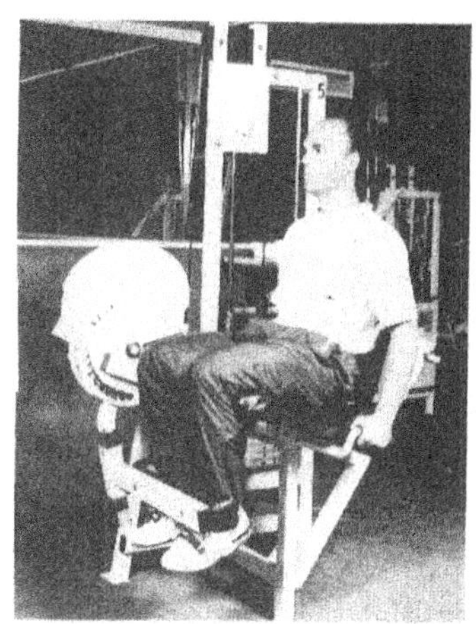

1

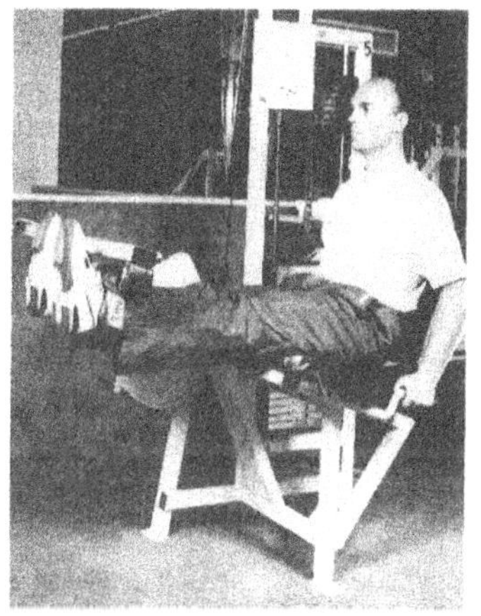

2

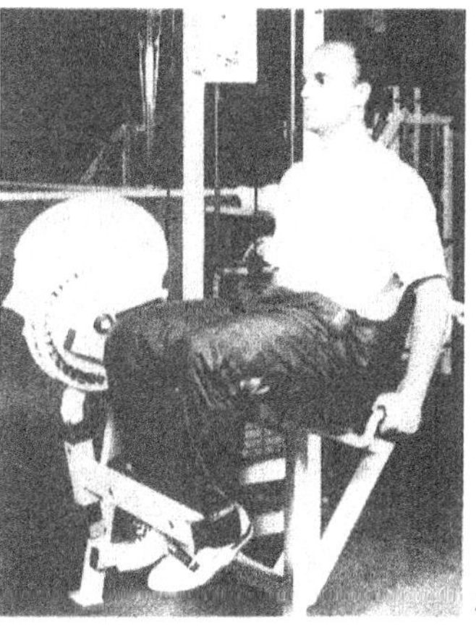

3

1

CALVES SITTING

1. Let the pressure take down the heel.
2. Push up with explosiveness and hold for one second.

2

3

1

2

3

BACK ONE-ARM ROW

1. Left knee on bench, with dumbbell in right hand. Back is straight.
2. Lift dumbbell in straight line up to side of chest.
3. Go down to start, remaining in control.

LEG CURL

1. Begin in ready position.
2. Curl with control to maximum. Don't change positions.
3. Return to start with control.

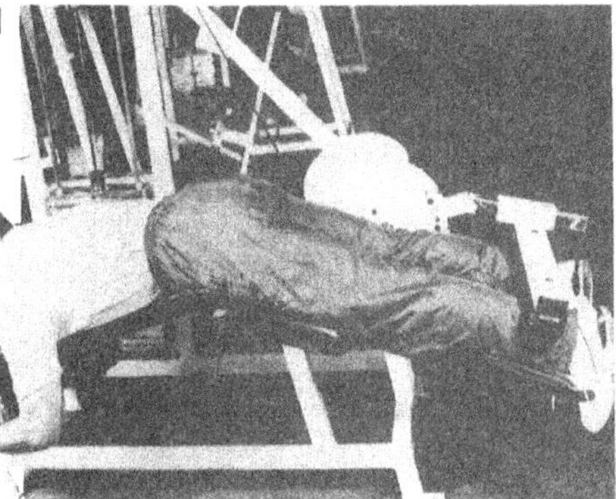
1

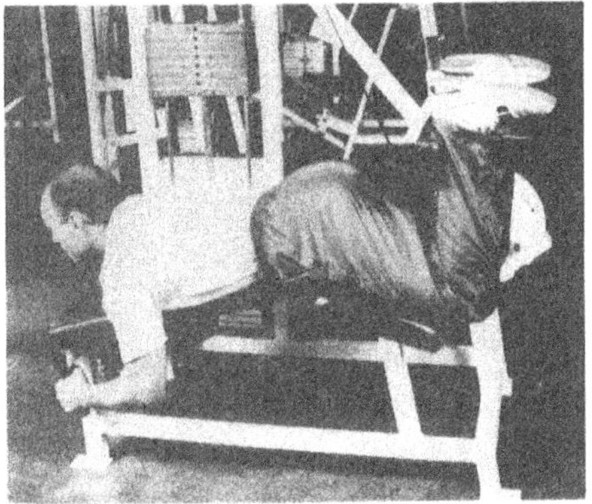
2

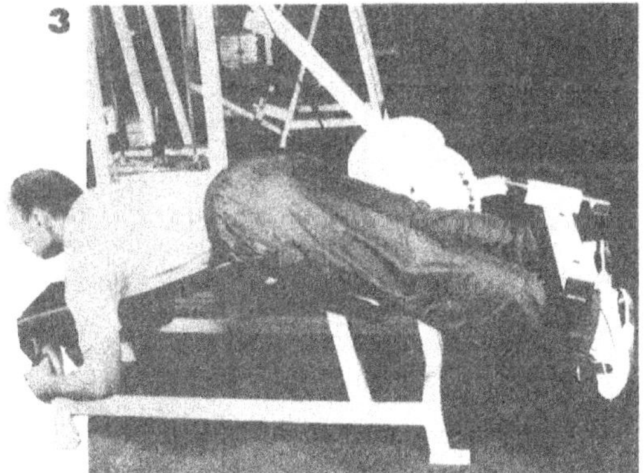
3

1

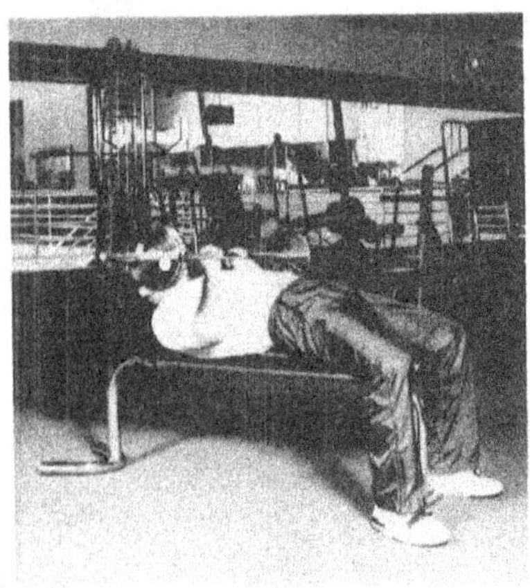

2

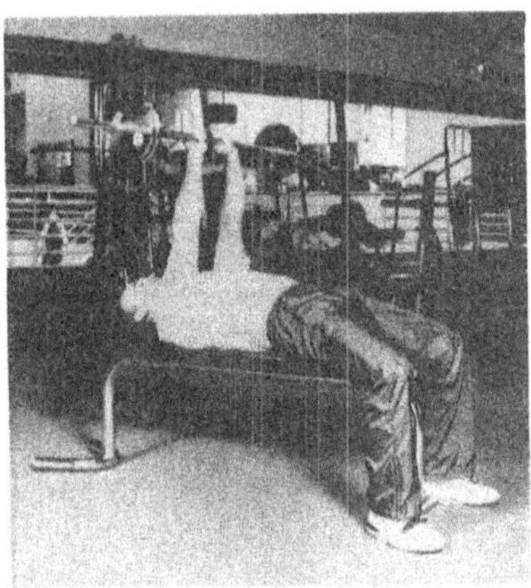

3

4

CLOSE-GRIP BENCH

1. On flat bench close grip on bar six inches between hands.
2. Go down with control. Hold elbows in and stop at solar plexus level.
3. Push straight up with power and explosiveness.
4. A close look at the grip of hands on bar.

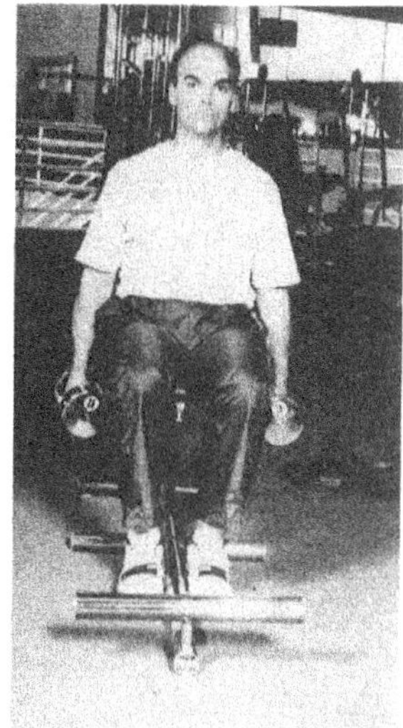

1

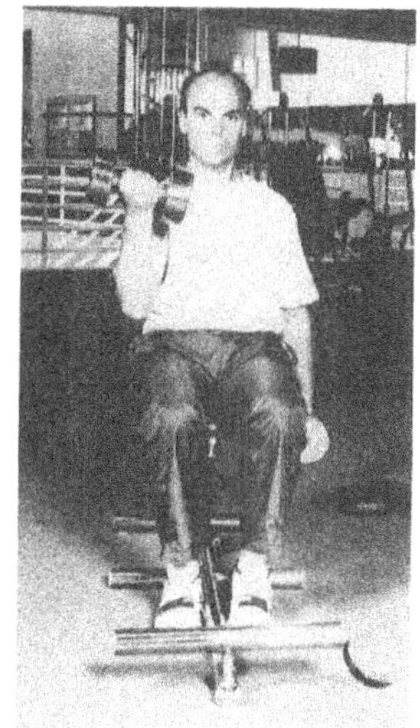

3

BICEPS SITTING ALTERNATE CURL

1. Sit holding dumbbells on sides.
2. Start lifting as right hand twists weight.
3. Keep lifting to maximum. Twist to straight palm facing chest. Elbow in

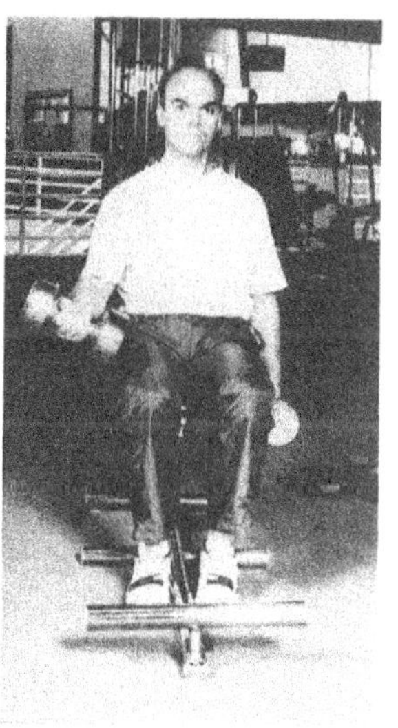

2

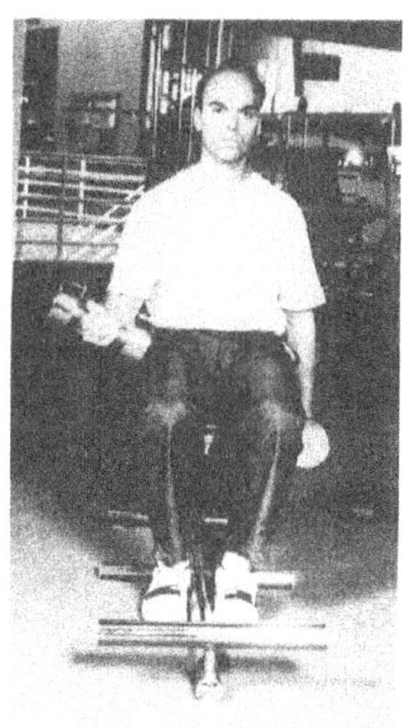

4

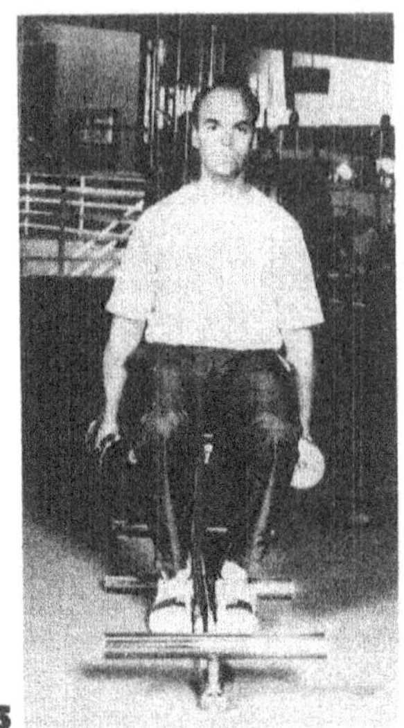

5

7

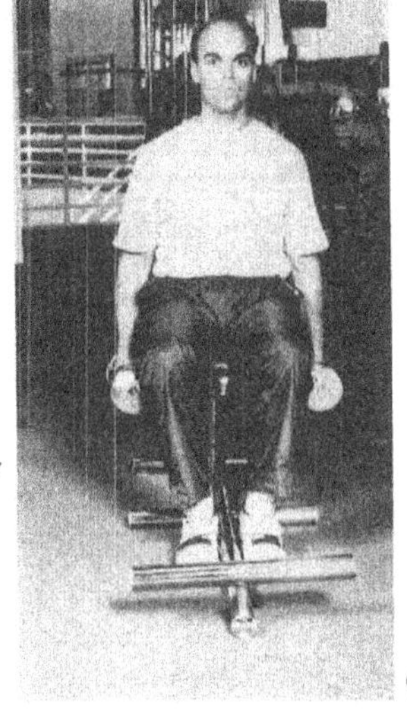

9

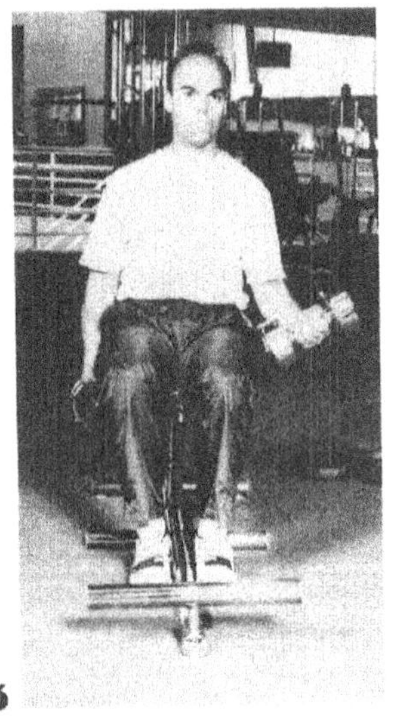

6

8

5. Return to starting position.
6. Start lifting left hand, twisting out.
7. Keep lifting to maximum, twist to straight palm facing chest. Elbow in.
8. Start going down.
9. Return to starting position.

CHAPTER 6

Concentration and Visualization

One of the hardest things for a competitor to do is stand in front of thousands of people and execute a form as though he was alone in the training hall at midnight with the doors locked.

I know. Last year as part of an exhibition in Paris, France, I performed a difficult and very personal kata in front of 24,000 people at Bercy Stadium.

Despite an appreciative crowd which could not help but make plenty of noise, I had to pretend I was doing the form sans audience in my living room. Later, as I spoke to the many martial arts aficionado, they remarked that they were most impressed by my ability to disregard outside influences. They said I moved as if I couldn't see or hear anyone.

In a way they were right. I admit that when I first started competing on the local level in Canada, the slightest distraction was enough to break my concentration. Someone would clap and I'd move my head. A loud voice would be greeted with a blink of the eye or stumble in my step. Fighters can get away with a lack of concentration and visualization. But as a forms competitor, you have to literally visualize an opponent across from you.

As I became more experienced I began to practice a series of special concentration and visualization exercises designed to keep me from letting the things get between me and my form.

It doesn't take much, really, except time and practice. My favorite moments come alone my living room. I assume a zazen, or Japanese meditation stance, by sitting on the back of my heels and concentrating on a single point in front of me. There is no blinking of the eyes or twisting of the shoulders. It is quiet, still and I am breathing so, so easy. I envision myself doing the form, each step as smooth and as flowing as a ripple of water.

Close your eyes and see the perfect performance, almost as if you had put a videotape in your head and were watching it from a distance.

You'll be surprised that the next time you hit the floor, with a crowd watching from the stands and competitors walking all about, you'll be able to revert back to that private moment. Suddenly, the form, the floor and you are one. It's a great feeling, one which surely won't get past the judges.

CHAPTER 7

The Cardiovascular Pump-Up

There are three or four nationally rated tournaments every year that draw the top-ranked performers on the circuit. Although the competition usually is keen, one forms and fighting practitioner will stand out and easily eclipse the field.

But every once is a while, the field iswideopen. I remember one East Coast national that still has martial artists and judges shaking their collective heads. Not only did the event draw the cream of the crop from across the United States and Europe, but for one very special weekend it appeared as though every forms and fighting competitor was giving the performance of his life.

Survival of the fittest is one thing. This was a survival of the fittest of the fittest. I was entered in the open forms division and in the preliminaries alone, there were six ties among the top ten finishers. I was one of three tied for first; we all had to do a second form.

After the first extra round a tie remained between two of us. We were forced to do a third form—three forms in a little under 15 minutes, each showing the same excellence in execution, strength, focus, balance and power.

Although both of us were highly skilled, seasoned competitors, with a host of such run-offs under our belts, I eventually endured because I was in better condition. My opponent, who turned in two great performances, floundered on his final attempt because he ran out of gas, pure and simple.

The secret to my success? A comprehensive training program that included plenty of cardiovascular work for just such an occasion. I realized long ago that the talent around the country is just too good week in and week out; if I was going to survive the big events, which in most cases featured plenty of ties, then I needed to supplement my regular workout with endurance training. Usually, if you take two people with the same talent level, the one with better endurance will come out on top. In the end, his forms are crisp and clean, while the other's look sloppy and disjointed.

A cardiovascular program greatly depends on the tools you have at your disposal. If your training hall is equipped with a heavy bag, Lifecycle and

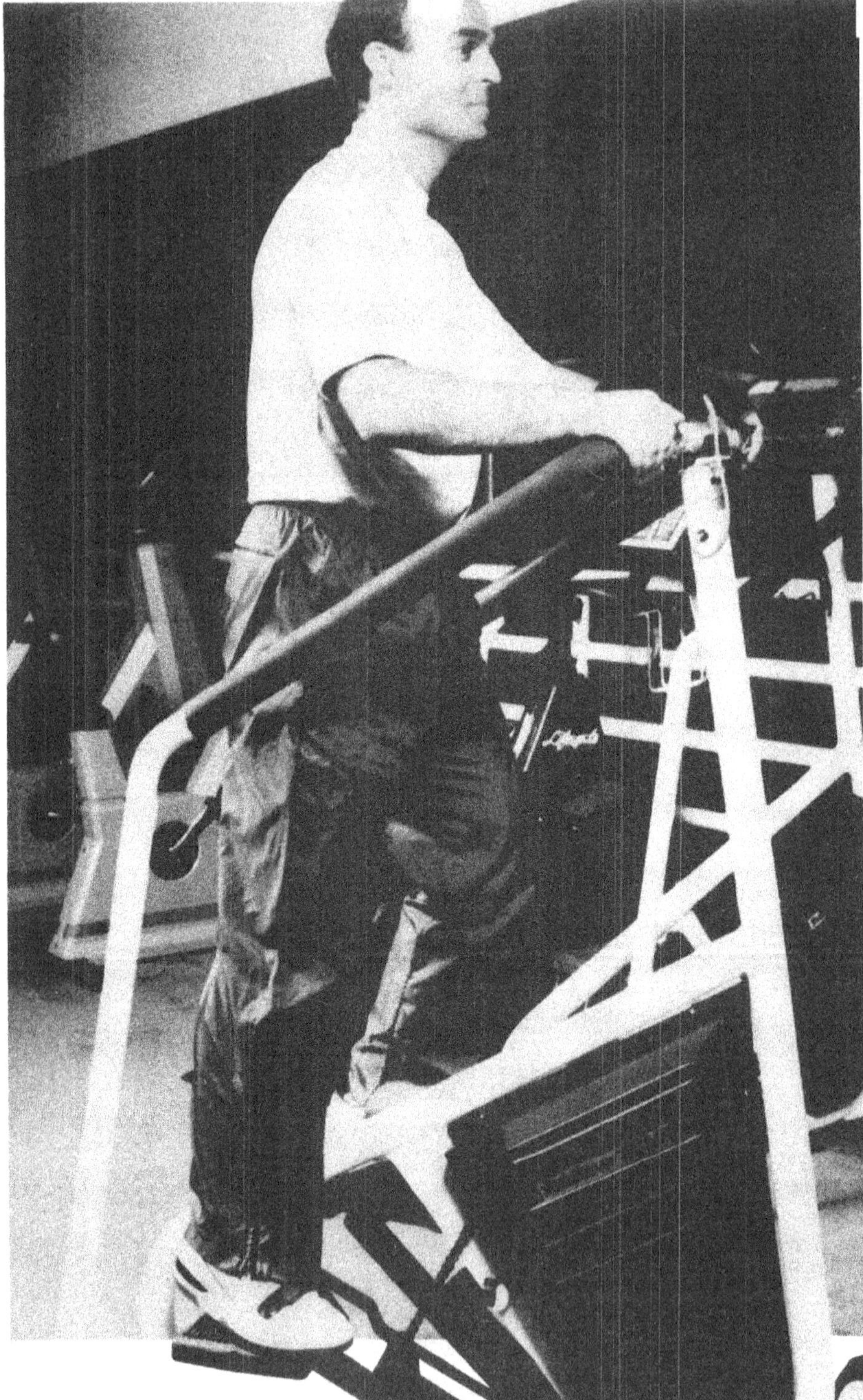

StairMaster, you're in great shape. If not, plan on doing plenty of running, biking and jump roping. (A full workout schedule is included as part of my three-, five- and six-day training program in Chapter 9.)

The best advice is to start slow and build according to your limits. As I already have stated, listen closely to your body. It will tell you when enough is enough. Also, vary your routine to prevent boredom.

If you are a forms competitor, practice two or even three forms as though a championship depended on your performance. That means taking only a three-to-five minute break between exercises. If sparring is your game, shadowbox and shadow kick three rounds, rest a minute, do three more rounds and then rest again.

Fans of boxing will note that in most major fights the pugilists appear evenly match through the first few rounds. But during periods four-through-six, the boxer in the best shape begins to prevail. Why? Because he has maintained a strict cardiovascular training program that allows him to continue when his opponent has said, "No mas."

CARDIOVASCULAR

STAIRMASTER

1. Step, in position to push with left leg.
2. Left leg steps strongly downward.
3. Left leg goes to maximum, right Is up.
4. Do this exercise regularly with explosiveness.

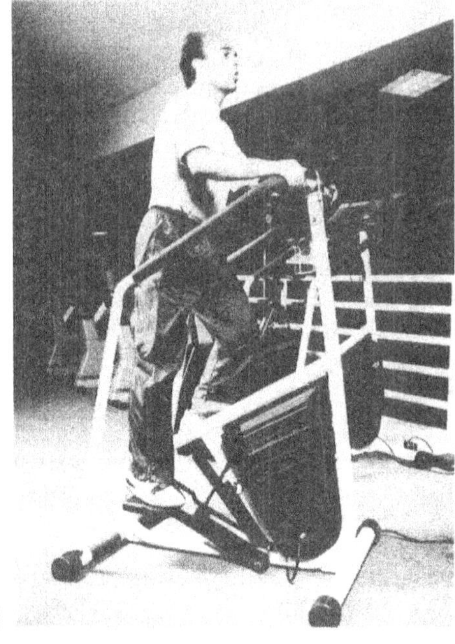

1

2

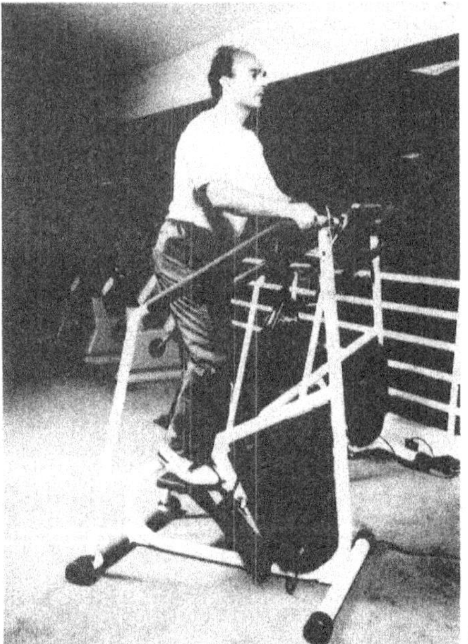

3

ECYCLE OR CYCLING

Loft leg Is up.

Motion begins, with left knee pushing downward and right knee going up.

Romain Intense and work to maximum.

1

2

RUNNING (INDOORS OR OUTDOORS)

1. Right log Is stepping (pushing). Loft leg moving forward. Keep arm motion opposite knee.
2. Same as photo one, but using other leg.
3. Right leg Is leading smoothly for next foot

1

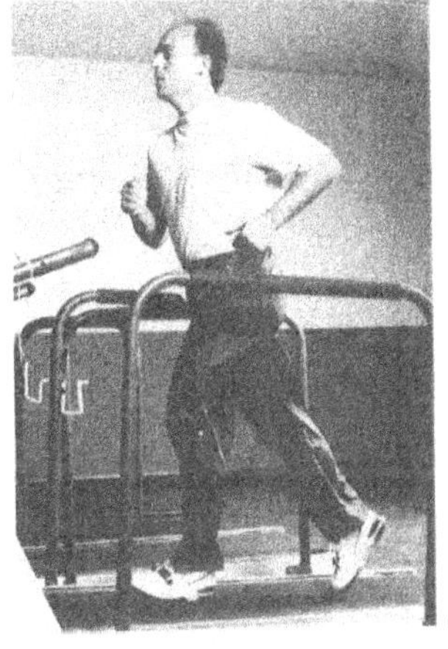

2

3

1

4

2

5

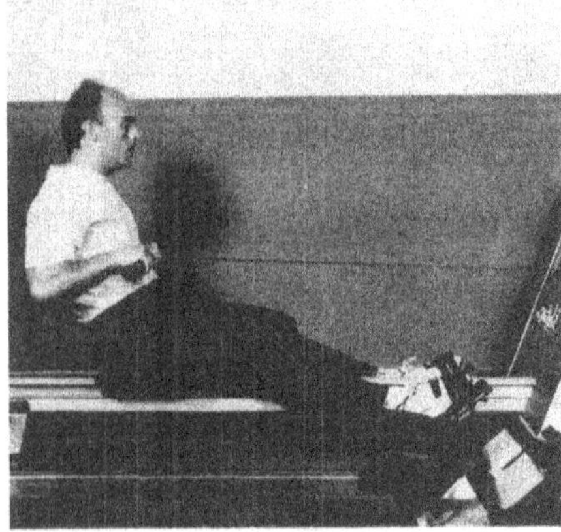
3

ROWING MACHINE

1. Starting position.
2. As leg is pushing, keep back and arm straight.
3. Extend leg and pull arms back to midsection.
4. Return with control.
5. Return to finish position ready to be firm. Be consistent.

CHAPTER 8

The Diet of Champions

Proper diet often is the most neglected aspect of a martial artist's overall training program. Because of a practitioner's myriad and oftentimes strenuous workout regimen, a diet that provides both energy and stamina is paramount to success. When I was younger, I never gave diet much consideration. As with most kids, I ate whatever I wanted, whenever I wanted with little or no regard to its affect on my system. Food is food, I thought, what's could be the problem?

But as I got older and began competing on a regular basis, I learned that some of the foods I most enjoyed were doing the least amount of good. And it was not only what I was eating, but when I was eating that gave me trouble.

After speaking with many top champions on the national circuit, I discovered those who competed on a regular basis regarded diet as being equally as important as any other segment of their total training program.

Now don't worry: This is not one of those drop-20-pounds-in-20-days diets. The idea is not to lose weight, but rather to keep your body performing at peak efficiency, both between tournaments and during competition. This is a comprehensive health program that will make you more fit and full of energy.

In many cases, what you don't eat is as important as what you put into your body. After years of experimentation, I have found that fatty, greasy foods are hard to digest and make you feel sluggish. When the body is working at less than 100 percent, your training will suffer.

My breakfast meal remains virtually the same, whether or not I'm training for competition. I try to stay away from greasy or fried foods such as eggs and bacon. I prefer something light, like hard-boiled eggs (stay away from the yolk), whole grain cereals with low-fat milk, fruit, two slices of bread and granola bars. Honey and sugar is fine in moderation. I wash it down with fruit juice and two glasses of water. Coffee is a no-no.

My lunch and dinner menus are interchangeable and since my meals are not fattening, I can eat as much as I want. The best foods include salads, rice, chicken, horse meat (if you can get it) or fish with steamed vegetables. Two or three times per week—especially before a tournament—you also should add pasta to your diet. A hard training schedule depletes your body of the necessary carbohydrates. Pasta, with natural tomato sauce (no meat sauce), will replenish those carbs. Again, chase it down with fruit juices or two glasses of water.

Jell-O, fruit (any melon because of the natural sugar) or granola bars are perfect for dessert. Try to stay away from ice cream.

During a competition, since you never know when you'll be called upon to perform, what you eat must be digestible within 30 minutes-to-one hour. Also, most arenas and gyms favor the fast-food approach, so your best bet is to bring your favorite munchies from home. Fruits and granola bars, plus an ample supply of water, should keep you going. Afterward, head for the pasta bar for another dose of carbohydrates.

One of the more annoying aspects of competing on the national level is the nervousness you'll feel when your division is called. Diet will play an important role in how your body reacts to this queasy feeling. Foods not easily digestible will make their presence felt as you prepare for competition.

Changing your diet shows you have made a commitment to feeling better. And it's been proven that the better you feel, the better you'll perform.

WHAT TO EAT

Breakfast:

- Whole grain cereals with low-fat milk • Yogurt
- 2 slices of bread (With a little butter or honey) • Fruit juice
- Hard-boiled or scrambled eggs • 2 glasses of water
  (Nothing fried) • Banana

Lunch and Dinner (Interchangeble):

- Salad (With tuna or chicken added)
- 8 ounces of meat (Chicken, veal, fish, horse meat or beef liver) not fried
- Pasta (As much as you want, but with natural tomato sauce)
- Rice
- Steamed vegetables
- Fruit juice
- 2 glasses of water

Dessert:

- Fruit (Especially melons) • Granola bars • Jell-0

Tournament Diet:

- Night Before — Pasta (A lot, until 4 hours before competition)
- Morning Of — Orange juice, two slices of raisin bread, apple sauce and lots of water
- During — Fruit, dry raisins, fruit juice, granola bars, brand muffins)
- Lunch or Dinner — Vegetable juice, mixed salad, cottage cheese, dry raisins, bread or bagel with a bit of butter
- After — Lots of water, increase potassium intake, add salt to your food and plenty of pasta (with natural tomato sauce)

YOGURT

CHAPTER 9

Your Weekly Training Schedule

BEGINNERS TRAINING SCHEDULE (3 Days Per Week)

Monday, Wednesday:

Regular martial arts training and pre- and post-class stretching

Friday:

Stretching	15 Minutes
Kicking	15 Minutes
Jump Rope	2 Sets of 3 Minutes
or Running	20 Minutes
Bag Punch and Kick	3 Minutes
Push-Ups	2 Sets of 20 (Regular)
	2 Sets of 20 (Large)
	Set of 15 (Extra Large)
Abdominals	2 Sets of 25 (Regular)
	2 Sets of 20 (Crunches)
	1 Set of Maximum (Touch Toes)

INTERMEDIATE TRAINING SCHEDULE (4 Days Per Week)

Monday, Wednesday, Thursday:

Regular martial arts training and pre- and post-class stretching

Tuesday:

See weight training schedule, plus 20 minutes on the bicycle. Also:

Jump Rope	3 Sets of 3 Minutes
or	20 Minutes of Running
Bag Punch or Kick	2 Sets of 3 Minutes
Shadow Kick and Punch	2 Sets of 3 Minutes

ADVANCED TRAINING SCHEDULE (6 Days Per Week)

Monday-Saturday:

Regular martial arts training and pre- and post-class stretching

Monday, Wednesday, and Friday morning:

Follow accompanying weight training schedule along with 30 minutes on the bike.

Tuesday, Thursday, and Saturday morning:

Running	20 Minutes
Jump Rope	5 Sets of 3 Minutes
Shadowboxing	2 Sets of 3 Minutes
Shadow Kicking	2 Sets of 3 Minutes
Bag Punching	2 Sets of 3 Minutes
Bag Kicking	2 Sets of 3 Minutes

Sunday:

Day off, but free to work out moderately.

1

1

2

2

▲

PUSH-UPS

REGULAR (30 reps per set)

1. Shoulder width.
2. Go down.

3

◀

MEDIUM (20 reps per set)

1. Six inches on each side.
2. Go midway.
3. Go all the way down.

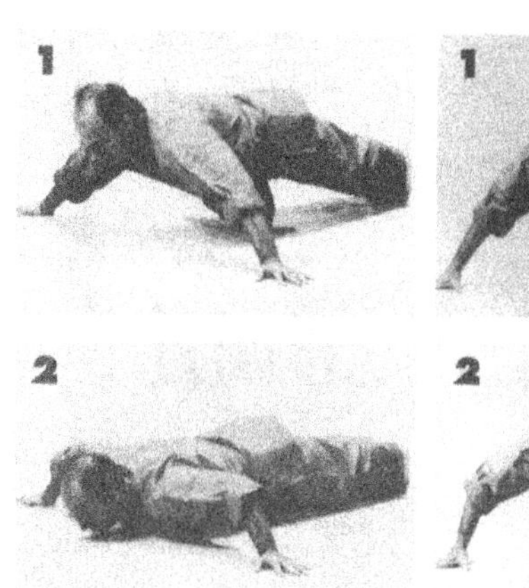

LARGE (15 reps per set)

1. Feet apart more on each side.
2. Go down.
3. Push yourself back up.

HI-LOW (20 reps per set)

1. Right hand high, left low.
2. Go halfway.
3. Go all the way.

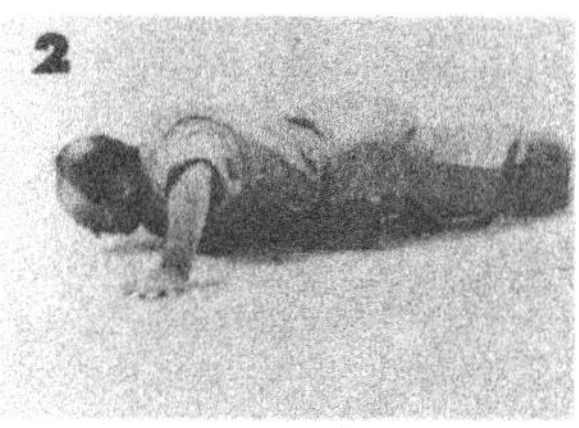

HI-LOW REVERSE (20 reps per set)

1. Left hand high, right low.
2. Go halfway.
3. Go all the way.

1

CLOSE (15 reps per set)

1. Hands together, thumb and index finger touching in center in line with sternum.
2. Go halfway.

2

3

CHAPTER 10

Jean Frenette Up Close and Personal

Several years ago during an exhibition and competition in Sun City, South Africa, Jean Frenette offered his unique teaching services to 25 dancers who were performing as part of a musical revue appearing at one of the resort's hotels.

These dancers were in their second year of a worldwide tour, which included two shows a night, six nights a week, 50 weeks a year. To say they were fit physically would be an understatement; still, Frenette said he saw something in their performance he thought he could improve through his personal stretching and kicking routine.

The dancers scoffed at the notion, but one morning during rehearsal, Frenette appeared on stage and took some of the dancers aside. Within seconds he assumed a splits position. Minutes later, the group was on the floor, taking its cue from the Canadian-born forms champion.

They were hooked, and for the next 30 minutes Frenette took the dancers on a magical tour of their bodies, showing them new ways to put more bounce in those old, tired steps.

The dancers left feeling sore and tired, but at the same time exhilarated at the prospect of learning something that would make them jump, kick and move better than ever before. As expected, Jean Frenette had gained a new set of converts.

And it's been this way since the mid-1970s, when a then-unknown Frenette exploded onto the scene by winning his first junior championship in Montreal, Quebec. He followed his domination of the junior circuit by capturing the Quebec adult forms championship in 1980. The overall Canadian forms trophy has had his name on it since 1981.

Since his sudden emergence more than a decade ago, Jean Frenette has been the standard by which forms excellence is judged. His performances around the world have been met with a steady stream of standing ovations and cries of "encore."

A Montreal native, Jean has been rated in the top 10 in martial arts forms since 1983, twice garnering the coveted top position. Voted to the *Inside Karate Hall* of Fame in 1988, Frenette has won hundreds of tournament forms grand championships. His crowning achievements include four consecutive World Amateur Karetedo Association (WAKO) Championships (he was favored to win No. 5 in 1991), the 1985 Bermuda Open Forms Grand Championships, and the 1986 South African Open Forms Grand Championship.

A member of the world-famous Transworld Oil Karate team, Jean's considered a folk hero in Europe and Russia, where his seminars and exhibitions have drawn millions. A recent exhibition in Paris drew more than 24,000 appreciative spectators to Bercy Stadium.

His amazing talents have led to numerous roles on screen and in television. Among his over 40 screen credits are work on all six *Police Academy monies,* a co-starring role in the recently released *Scanners 3, Sadie and Son,* starring Debbie Reynolds, and stunt work on *Speed Zone* (formerly *Cannonball Run III).* He also has appeared as a guest on several Canadian soap operas and "Knightwatch," an action series produced by Fox television.

Founder of the Sankudo International Karatedo Organization, with a current membership of more than 10,000, Frenette's three-part videotape stretching series for Panther Productions remains one of the company's hottest sellers.

His first book for Unique Publications, *Jean Frenette's Complete Guide to Stretching,* became an overnight sensation.

Clearly, the rest of the world has discovered what 25 doubting dancers in South Africa learned on a barren stage floor—when it comes to the myriad talents of Jean Frenette, seeing is believing.

JEAN FRENETTE'S CHAMPIONSHIP HONOR ROLL

- W.A.K.O. World Championships (1987, 1988, 1989, 1990)
- AKA Grand Nationals
- U.S. Top Ten Nationals
- U.S. Capitol Classics
- Boston Nationals
- Atlantic Grand Slam
- Diamond Nationals
- Battle of Atlanta
- U.S. Open
- Bermuda Invitational
- Blue Grass Nationals
- South African Games
- **Canadian Games**

1
3
OLYMPIAHALLE
2
2

JEAN
FRENETTE
Karten erhältich in allen Raiffeisenkassen
Stadt Reisebüro
Eintritt S 80,-
Tir Landesreisebüro
9.OKTOBER 16^00
kongresshaus innsbruck
EM Profi - Kampf KICKBOXEN
FRANZ HALLER (I) - MICHEL MANGEOT (F)
WM Revanche - Kampf TAE KWON DO
JOHN COCU (NL) - EGON MEIER (JU)
Raiffeisen.
Die Bank

www.ingramcontent.com/pod-product-compliance
Lightning Source LLC
LaVergne TN
LVHW020641100826
845148LV00012B/2289

9780934489966